Steck-Vaughn

Language

Exercises

Book 4

Harcourt Achieve

Rigby • Saxon • Steck-Vaughn

www.HarcourtAchieve.com
1.800.531.5015

Acknowledgments

Illustrations: P. 22 Michael Krone

Photography: P. 18 Rick Williams; p. 31 Cooke Photographics; p. 43 Michael Dwyer/Stock Boston; pp. 44, 48, Cooke Photographics.

Additional photography by Comstock Royalty Free; PictureQuest Royalty Free; Photodisc/Getty Royalty Free; Royalty-Free/CORBIS.

Macmillan/McGraw-Hill School Publishing Company: Pronunciation Key, reprinted with permission of the publisher, from *Macmillan School Dictionary 1.* Copyright © 1990 Macmillan Publishing Company, a division of Macmillan, Inc.

LANGUAGE EXERCISES Series:

Book 1	Book 4	Book 7
Book 2	Book 5	Book 8
Book 3	Book 6	Review

ISBN 978-1-4190-1872-5   ISBN 1-4190-1872-8

6 7 8   0982   12 11

4500295074

Table of Contents

Unit 5 Composition

Unit 6 Study Skills

Final Reviews

A. Write **S** before each pair of synonyms, **A** before each pair of antonyms, and **H** before each pair of homonyms.

_____ **1.** good, bad   _____ **3.** big, large

_____ **2.** their, they're   _____ **4.** begin, start

B. Circle the correct definition for the underlined word in the sentence.

1. The snap made me look around.

sound made with fingers   a metal fastener

C. Write **P** before each word with a prefix, **S** before each word with a suffix, and **C** before each compound word.

_____ **1.** careless   _____ **3.** baseball

_____ **2.** misbehave   _____ **4.** reuse

D. Write a contraction for the underlined words.

_____ **1.** He will not go.   _____ **2.** I am tired.

E. Write **D** before the declarative sentence, **IM** before the imperative sentence, **E** before the exclamatory sentence, and **IN** before the interrogative sentence.

_____ **1.** That is a great shirt!   _____ **3.** I think it fits just fine.

_____ **2.** Can't you see that it's too big?   _____ **4.** Take it back to the store.

F. Draw a line between the subject and the predicate. Underline the simple subject once and the simple predicate twice.

1. It is raining outside.
2. There are puddles in the street.

G. Combine the sentences into one sentence.

Jerry went out to dinner. He went to the new restaurant.

_____

_____

H. Separate the run-on sentence.

Alex cooked a big meal, he served it to his friends.

_____

_____

I. Underline the common nouns, and circle the proper nouns in the sentence.

Betty chose two dogs, Yip and Yap, to take home to her children.

J. Write the correct possessive noun to complete the sentence.

The mailbox has a flag. The _____ flag is up.

K. Write **A** if the underlined verb is an action verb, **L** if it is a linking verb, or **H** if it is a helping verb.

_____ **1.** Cyclone ran the race in record time.

_____ **2.** After a rain the air smells clean.

_____ **3.** We are walking daily for exercise.

L. Write **past**, **present**, or **future** to show the tense of each underlined verb.

_____ **1.** They will need more ice soon.

_____ **2.** Lee told his friend the truth.

_____ **3.** She saves forty dollars a month.

M. Circle the correct verb in each sentence.

1. Soccer (is, are) a popular sport today.   **2.** Many fans will (come, came) to watch.

N. Complete each sentence by writing the correct pronoun for the words in parentheses.

1. Yesterday (Anika and I) _____ went to the library.

2. Then we met (our friends) _____ at the theater.

O. In the sentence below, underline each adjective, and circle each adverb.

We carefully planned an exciting surprise party for Henry.

P. Circle the correct word to complete each sentence.

1. No one (never, ever) comes to visit us.

2. (Them, Those) people (don't, doesn't) know what they're missing!

2

Q. In the letter below, underline letters that should be capitalized, and add punctuation where needed.

977 n seaside dr

ann arbor mi 68445

jan 25 2006

dear kathleen

mario and i took ginger to the vet to get her shots ___ she really hates to go ___

how is frisky ___ i hope you are both fine ___

your friend

elena

R. Rewrite the sentences below in paragraph form. Put the topic sentence first, and circle the time order words.

1. Then we spoke to the neighbors.
2. We just moved into a new house.
3. Finally, we had peace and quiet.
4. First, the dog next door began barking all night.

_____

_____

_____

_____

S. Using the words and phrases below, fill in the outline.

Name and number   Information needed from caller
Taking a phone message   Message

Statement: _____

    I. _____

       A. _____

       B. _____

T. Use the dictionary entry below to answer the questions.

bad (bad) *adj.* **1.** poor: *It was a bad copy.* **2.** evil: *He met a bad man.*
 3. spoiled: *The meat was bad.*

1. What part of speech is the word bad?

_____

n.	noun
pron.	pronoun
v.	verb
adj.	adjective
adv.	adverb
prep.	preposition

2. Would band or baby come before bad in the dictionary?

_____

3. Would bacon / bake or bag / band be the guide words for bad?

_____

U. Use the sample encyclopedia entry to answer the questions.

AUDUBON, JOHN JAMES (1785–1851) was an artist. He came to
North America in 1803 to study and draw birds. *See also*
AUDUBON SOCIETY.

1. Who is this article about? _____

2. What is the cross-reference? _____

Below is a list of the sections on *Check What You Know* and the
pages on which the skills in each section are taught. If you missed
any questions, turn to the pages listed, and practice the skills. Then
correct the problems you missed on *Check What You Know*.

Lesson 1

Synonyms

> ■ A **synonym** is a word that has the same or almost the same meaning as another word.
> EXAMPLES: last–final; leave–go; prize–award

A. For each underlined word, circle its synonym at the end of the sentence.

1. My goal is to become a biologist. (thought, desire)
2. I like going out into the field to study. (outdoors, lab)
3. The best learning comes through observing things in nature. (seeing, changing)
4. I record my findings in a journal. (write, tape)
5. Then I compare what I have seen to what books say. (question, match)
6. If there is a difference, I consult my teacher. (direct, ask)
7. Together we explore possible theories. (ideas, facts)
8. Sometimes there are only small differences between theories. (little, large)
9. I like studying plants the most. (enjoy, hate)
10. I raised some bean plants for an experiment. (grew, bought)
11. The experiment worked exactly as planned. (arranged, found)

B. Rewrite these sentences. Use synonyms from the box below for the underlined words.

active	brave	common	glad
halt	large	stay	uncommon

1. The ordinary hive has many worker bees.

   _____

2. It is not unusual to find 80,000 busy workers in a colony.

   _____

3. The fearless worker bee will do anything to stop the enemies of the hive.

   _____

4. The hive must remain warm, or the bees will die.

   _____

5. Farmers are happy to see big hives near their fields.

   _____

- An **antonym** is a word that has the opposite meaning of another word.   EXAMPLES: stop—go; yes—no; hot—cold

A. For each underlined word, write an antonym from the box.

1. <u>dull</u> knife   _____ knife

2. <u>hard</u> cheese   _____ cheese

3. <u>correct</u> answer   _____ answer

4. <u>spend</u> money   _____ money

5. <u>remember</u> groceries   _____ groceries

6. <u>neat</u> room   _____ room

7. <u>finish</u> chores   _____ chores

8. <u>old</u> clothes   _____ clothes

9. <u>bottom</u> line   _____ line

begin
forget
messy
new
save
sharp
soft
top
wrong

B. Rewrite the paragraph using an antonym for each underlined word.

The <u>little</u> game was that evening. Scott and Jeff wanted to wear <u>dirty</u> uniforms. They believed that looking <u>bad</u> to the other team would help them win. They <u>dirtied</u> their uniforms at the same time. They used bleach to <u>fade</u> the colors. When they finished <u>washing</u> the uniforms, they discovered they had been <u>right</u>. Their uniforms were now the <u>opposite</u> color as those of the other team!

_____

_____

_____

_____

_____

_____

_____

■ A **homonym** is a word that sounds like another word. However, it has a different meaning and is spelled differently.
   EXAMPLES: it's, its   their, there, and they're
   It's means "it is." **It's** a nice day.
   Its means "belonging to it." The dog hurt **its** leg.

   Their means "belonging to them." That is **their** house.
   There means "in or at that place." Put it **there**.
   They're means "they are." **They're** going to the game.

A. Write it's or its to complete each sentence.

1. The team starts _____ practice at noon.

2. The coach says _____ necessary to practice.

3. I don't believe the players think _____ fun to practice.

4. Others say _____ exciting to watch the game from the sidelines.

5. The team is proud of _____ record.

6. If the team does _____ job, it will win.

7. I think _____ still a month until the championship game.

8. The team thinks _____ chance for winning the championship is good.

9. However, _____ too early to know for sure.

B. Circle the correct homonym in each sentence.

1. (There, Their, They're) is no reason to believe something is wrong.

2. (There, Their, They're) only a few minutes late.

3. I'm sure (there, their, they're) fine and will be here soon.

4. You know (there, their, they're) habits.

5. Wherever they go, they get (there, their, they're) late.

6. (There, Their, They're) families are like that, too.

7. I don't understand why (there, their, they're) always late.

8. Maybe (there, their, they're) clocks are wrong!

■ Remember that a **homonym** is a word that sounds like another word. EXAMPLES: to, two, too   right, write   hear, here
To means "toward" or "to do something." Go **to** the store.
Two means "the number 2." Buy **two** gallons of milk.
Too means "also" or "more than enough." It's **too** hot.

Write means "to put words or numbers onto paper."
Did you **write** the letter?
Right means "correct" or "the opposite of left."
Turn **right** at the corner.

Hear means "listen." Didn't you **hear** me?
Here means "in this place." Meet me **here** in one hour.

A. Write to, two, or too to complete each sentence.

1. It was _____ years ago that José and I went on vacation _____ the mountains.

2. We thought about going back last year, _____, but we decided not _____.

3. We both thought going _____ the beach would be more fun.

4. Since only _____ of us were going, we thought we'd meet more people there.

B. Write right or write to complete each sentence.

1. I'll _____ directions for finding my house.

2. You'll need a map to find the _____ roads.

3. Go ten miles and turn _____ at the bridge.

4. You're on the _____ road if you pass the mall.

C. Write hear or here to complete each sentence.

1. "I can't _____ you because of the music," shouted Alan.

2. "Come _____ so I can _____ you better," said Peter.

3. "Why did we come _____ to talk? I can't _____ anything," said Alan.

4. "Let's get out of _____," said Peter.

Multiple Meanings

> ■ Some words have more than one meaning. They are spelled the same, and often are pronounced the same, but they mean different things. The only way to know the meaning of these words is to see how they are used in a sentence.
> EXAMPLES: I **can** go.   Get the **can** of beans.

A. Circle the correct meaning for each underlined word.

1. She put the pad behind her back and leaned against it.
   pillow   walk softly

2. A tear rolled down her cheek.
   rip or pull apart   salty liquid from the eye

3. The rain continued to beat against the little cabin.
   strike over and over   to mix

4. As she listened, the warning bell began to ring.
   make the sound of a bell   narrow circle of metal worn on the finger

5. The pounding waves made a terrible racket.
   light bat used in sports   loud noise

6. Her cabin would soon be lost to the storm.
   attack   heavy winds with rain or snow

7. Her only hope was that someone would come and lead her to safety.
   soft metal   guide

B. Write a sentence for each meaning of the words given.

1. wind: blowing air

   _____

   wind: to tighten the spring of

   _____

2. rock: to move back and forth

   _____

   rock: a large stone

   _____

Lesson 6

Prefixes

> ■ A **prefix** is a syllable added to the beginning of a word to change the meaning of the word.
> EXAMPLES:
> The prefix dis- means "not" or "the opposite of." **dis**appear
> The prefix mis- means "bad(ly)" or "wrong(ly)." **mis**behave
> The prefix re- means "again" or "back." **re**do
> The prefix un- means "not" or "the opposite of." **un**friendly

A. Complete each sentence by adding un- or dis- to the word in parentheses.

1. Tabor the Great made a man _____ from the stage. (appear)

2. The man looked _____ about what would happen to him. (concerned)

3. He seemed _____ that he was even on the stage. (aware)

4. The man vanished! The audience tried to _____ where he'd gone. (cover)

5. But the man reappeared and was _____. (harmed)

6. It would be hard to _____ an act as great as Tabor's. (like)

7. No one could _____ with the fact that it had been a fine evening. (agree)

B. Complete each sentence by adding mis- or re- to the word in parentheses.

1. I _____ the plan for the park at the edge of town. (understood)

2. I didn't want to see a _____ of such fine land. (use)

3. The plan is to _____ our town as it was long ago. (create)

4. It will help us to _____ the history of the town. (live)

5. I really _____ the plan. (judged)

6. I should learn not to _____ before I know all the facts. (act)

> ■ A **suffix** is a syllable added to the end of a word to change the meaning of the word.
>
> EXAMPLES:
>
> The suffix -ful means "full of," "able to," or "the amount that will fill." hope**ful**, help**ful**, spoon**ful**
>
> The suffix -less means "without" or "not able to do." hope**less**, harm**less**

A. In each blank, write the word that matches the definition in parentheses.

effortless	worthless	meaningful	endless
successful	careless	joyless	tireless

1. Giving a _____ party is not always easy. (full of success)

2. When planning a party, I am _____. (not able to tire)

3. If the party is well planned, it looks _____. (without effort)

4. A _____ mistake can ruin a party. (without care)

5. A _____ game helps people to get into the spirit of the party. (full of meaning)

6. There is an _____ number of party games. (without end)

7. But all of the planning is _____ if no one comes. (without worth)

8. It would be a _____ evening if no one came to my party! (without joy)

B. Write a definition for the underlined word in each phrase.

1. <u>colorless</u> soap _____ without color _____

2. <u>bottomless</u> pit _____

3. <u>sorrowful</u> event _____

4. <u>beautiful</u> car _____

5. <u>flavorless</u> meal _____

Compound Words

■ A **compound word** is a word formed by putting two or more words together.   EXAMPLES: railway, textbook

A. Write the two words that form each underlined compound word.

1. We are planning a picnic this <u>weekend</u>.

   _____   _____

2. Tess is bringing her delicious <u>homemade</u> chicken.

   _____   _____

3. My job is to bring the <u>watermelon</u>.

   _____   _____

4. The picnic will be over at <u>sunset</u>.

   _____   _____

**B. Combine words from the box to form compound words.
Use a compound word to complete each sentence.**

| fire | front | watch | speaker | water | boat | place | tug | man | loud |

1. The _____ inched slowly into the harbor.

2. The captain enjoyed looking at the buildings on the _____.

3. Using the _____, he called the crew to the deck.

4. As he waved to Mike, the night _____, he felt glad to be going home.

5. He would soon be home sitting in front of his warm _____.

C. Combine the words below to form four compound words. Use each word in a sentence of your own.

| news | night | note | base | mid | ball | paper | book |

1. _____   _____

2. _____   _____

3. _____   _____

4. _____   _____

Lesson 9

Contractions

> - A **contraction** is a word formed by joining two other words. When the two words are joined, a letter or letters are left out. An **apostrophe** (') is used to show where the missing letter or letters would be.
>   EXAMPLE: I ~~would~~—I'd   he ~~is~~—he's   we ~~have~~—we've
> - The only contraction that breaks this rule is won't. Won't means "will not." The i becomes o when the other letters are dropped.

A. Rewrite each sentence using a contraction for the words in parentheses.

1. (I will) need volunteers for the newspaper.

   _____

2. The first stories are due soon, so (we have) got to hurry.

   _____

3. (You will) each be given a section of the paper to work on.

   _____

4. Joyce says (she is) looking forward to the first copy.

   _____

5. Anthony says (he is) going to help us.

   _____

B. Underline the contraction in each sentence. Write the two words that make up each contraction.

1. Joe can't play in the basketball game tonight.

   _____   _____

2. He didn't remember to bring his uniform.

   _____   _____

3. The coach won't let him play without a uniform.

   _____   _____

4. Joe isn't happy about missing the game.

   _____   _____

5. No one thinks we'll win without Joe.

   _____   _____

Unit 1, Vocabulary

13

A. Rewrite each sentence using a synonym for each underlined word.

1. The <u>large</u> dog chewed on the <u>small</u> bone.

   _____

2. He was not <u>frightened</u> by the <u>strange</u> sight.

   _____

B. Find the pair of synonyms in each sentence. Write each pair on the lines.

1. She whispered the whole time, so we missed the entire movie.

   _____   _____

2. They built the house first, and then constructed the garage.

   _____   _____

C. Rewrite each sentence using an antonym for each underlined word.

1. The <u>tiny</u> fire is <u>cold</u>. _____

2. The <u>old</u> joke made me <u>cry</u>. _____

D. For each underlined word, circle the correct antonym at the end of the sentence.

1. It's hard to believe they could do such a <u>foolish</u> thing. (wise, funny)
2. It became a <u>funny</u> story to tell their friend. (sad, long)
3. The story did not <u>amuse</u> her, however. (entertain, sadden)

E. Circle the correct word or words to complete each sentence.

1. I can (hear, here) the speaker very clearly.
2. I have (to, too, two) tickets (to, too, two) this event.
3. (Its, It's) interesting to see the statue on (its, it's) stand.
4. She asked us to (write, right) our names the (write, right) way.
5. They expected to find (they're, their) workers already (there, their).

F. Circle the correct meaning of each underlined word.

1. The <u>wind</u> howled through the valley.

   to coil or turn   moving air

2. He watched the river <u>wind</u> on its way.

   to coil or turn   moving air

G. Write a sentence for the meaning given for each underlined word.

1. batter: person at bat

_____

batter: mixture for cooking

_____

2. duck: a water bird

_____

duck: lower the head

_____

H. Add mis-, dis-, re-, un-, -ful, or -less to the words in parentheses to complete each sentence.

1. I _____ (agree) with _____ (turning) books to the library late.

2. It is _____ (thought) to _____ (use) your right to the books.

3. Be _____ (thank) for _____ (limited) use of the library.

I. Combine words from the box to make compound words. Use the compound words to complete each sentence.

| air | cut | door | hair | conditioned | knob |

1. It felt nice and cool in the _____ store.

2. Richard's reflection told him it was time for a _____.

3. Jill turned the _____ slowly, and the door creaked open.

J. Underline the contractions in each sentence. Write the two words that make up each contraction.

1. I'd like to try mountain climbing, but I'm too scared.

_____   _____

2. As long as he's happy, it doesn't matter what job he has.

_____   _____

3. She didn't know what she'd do next.

_____   _____

A. Rewrite the paragraph using synonyms for each underlined word.

The little man carried a large suitcase. He seemed to be trying to locate someone. Suddenly an auto screeched to a halt. The man grinned when he saw his best friend in the car.

_____

_____

_____

_____

B. Complete the paragraph. Write the correct homonym in each space.

I have no choice. I'll have to stay home until Amanda gets

_____ (here, hear). Jeff is _____

(to, too, two) young _____ (to, too, two) be left alone.

_____ (There They're, Their) is no one else to watch

him. _____ (Its, It's) wrong for you to think I'd leave a

child who's _____ (to, too, two) years old alone. I'll

wait to _____ (here, hear) from Amanda. Until then,

_____ (there, they're, their) just going to have to

get along without me. I know this is the _____

(write, right) thing to do.

C. Read the definitions of each word. Then write one sentence for each meaning given.

1. brush: tool for painting

_____

brush: bushes

_____

2. fly: insect

_____

fly: move through the air with wings

_____

D. Use mis-, dis-, un-, or -ful with one of the underlined words in each sentence to form a new word. Rewrite each sentence using the new word. Be sure the sentence keeps the same meaning.

1. I am <u>not happy</u> with the way the tape sounds.

_____

2. I was <u>full of hope</u> that this tape would be good.

_____

3. Now it seems that I <u>wrongly judged</u> it.

_____

4. I'm still <u>not satisfied</u> with the way it sounds.

_____

E. Combine the words below to form three compound words. Then use each word in a sentence of your own.

camp	post	light	fire	card	flash

1. _____

_____

2. _____

_____

3. _____

_____

F. Underline all of the contractions in the paragraph. Then write each contraction and the two words from which it is made.

> There isn't much I wouldn't do for my grandmother. She's the most wonderful person I know. She lives with us now because she can't take care of herself. But her wise words help everyone in our family, and we're all glad to have her here.

1. _____   _____   _____

2. _____   _____   _____

3. _____   _____   _____

4. _____   _____   _____

5. _____   _____   _____

> ■ A **sentence** is a group of words that expresses a complete thought.
>
> EXAMPLES: Ralph washed the car. He drove to the store.

A. Write S on the line if the group of words is a sentence.

_____ 1. Sarah ran to the car.

_____ 2. She was in a big hurry.

_____ 3. All of a sudden.

_____ 4. Sarah stared at the car.

_____ 5. She couldn't believe her eyes.

_____ 6. Three of the tires.

_____ 7. Were completely flat.

_____ 8. Sarah had no idea what caused the flats.

_____ 9. Up the driveway toward the house.

_____ 10. An open box of nails.

B. Write S on the line if the group of words is a sentence. If it is not a sentence, rewrite it as a sentence by adding whatever is needed.

1. The parents' club has its monthly meeting tonight.

_____

2. All of the parents.

_____

3. A slide show about fire drills will be shown.

_____

4. Following the slide show.

_____

5. The parents will take information home.

_____

Declarative and Interrogative Sentences

> - A sentence that makes a statement is called a **declarative sentence.**   EXAMPLE: We have two dogs.
> - A sentence that asks a question is called an **interrogative sentence.**   EXAMPLE: Do you have a dog?

A. Write <u>declarative</u> if the sentence makes a statement. Write <u>interrogative</u> if the sentence asks a question.

_____ **1.** How are you today?

_____ **2.** You didn't look well yesterday.

_____ **3.** I hope you're not getting sick.

_____ **4.** Are you getting enough rest?

_____ **5.** You really can't afford to get sick.

_____ **6.** Isn't the big game this week?

_____ **7.** You need to be healthy for this game.

_____ **8.** Will you be here tomorrow?

_____ **9.** We are going to have a practice before the game.

_____ **10.** Are you ready for the game?

_____ **11.** Did you practice much?

_____ **12.** I practiced a lot.

_____ **13.** Do you think the practice will help?

_____ **14.** I get so nervous about big games.

_____ **15.** How do you stay so calm?

_____ **16.** Will you help me practice?

_____ **17.** I could use some help.

_____ **18.** You're really a good friend.

B. Write one declarative sentence and one interrogative sentence about sports.

1. _____

2. _____

Changing Sentences

> ■ A statement can be made into a question by changing the order of the words in the sentence.   EXAMPLE: You are going to the show. Are you going to the show?
>
> ■ Sometimes a question word like <u>who</u>, <u>why</u>, <u>what</u>, <u>does</u>, or <u>how</u> must also be added to the statement to change it to a question.   EXAMPLE: The show is two hours long. How long is the show?

A. Turn each statement into a question by changing the order of the words.

1. I am finished. _____

2. You shouldn't be finished. _____

3. This is taking too long. _____

4. You are leaving. _____

5. You can stay. _____

B. Turn the statements below into questions. You may change the order of the words and add question words as needed.

1. Joe starts his new job today.

_____

2. He begins at nine o'clock.

_____

3. He will leave home at eight o'clock.

_____

4. Joe likes to work on cars.

_____

5. Repairing cars is very interesting.

_____

6. Joe is sure he will like this job.

_____

7. Joe will do a good job.

_____

Imperative and Exclamatory Sentences

> ■ A sentence that gives a command is called an **imperative sentence.**
>   EXAMPLES: Sit down. Read your book.
> ■ A sentence that shows surprise or emotion is called an **exclamatory sentence.**
>   EXAMPLES: Oh, you scared me! We won the game!

A. Write imperative if the sentence gives a command. Write exclamatory if the sentence shows surprise or emotion.

_____	**1.** You go first, Jack.
_____	**2.** Tell me if it's safe.
_____	**3.** I'm scared!
_____	**4.** Keep your voice down.
_____	**5.** I can't see!
_____	**6.** I'm lost!
_____	**7.** Be quiet.
_____	**8.** Come down here, Pete.
_____	**9.** I'm falling!
_____	**10.** Hurray, I'm out!
_____	**11.** Close the window.
_____	**12.** Watch out for that car.

B. Pretend that you are walking with a friend in a deep, dark forest. Write three imperative sentences and three exclamatory sentences.

1. _____

2. _____

3. _____

4. _____

5. _____

6. _____

Lesson 14

Subjects and Predicates

> ■ Every sentence has two parts. The **subject** of a sentence tells who or what the sentence is about. The **predicate** tells what the subject does or what happens to the subject.
> EXAMPLE: The marching band won the state championship.
> **Subject**—The marching band; **Predicate**—won the state championship

A. Add a subject to each predicate to make a sentence.

1. _____ play tennis. 3. _____ returned the ball.

2. _____ run. 4. _____ won the game.

B. Add a predicate to each subject to make a sentence.

1. Players _____. 3. Coaches _____.

2. Some fans _____. 4. Judges _____.

C. Write subject or predicate to tell which part of each sentence is underlined.

_____ 1. Tennis is a game.

_____ 2. It is played with a racket.

_____ 3. The player swings the racket.

_____ 4. A ball is also needed.

_____ 5. Two or four players may play at one time.

_____ 6. Love means zero points in tennis.

_____ 7. A set is won in six games.

D. Draw one line under each subject and two lines under each predicate.

1. Tennis was invented by Major Walter Wingfield.
2. The game was called tennis-on-the-lawn.
3. Mary Outerbridge brought the game to the United States.
4. Tennis is a popular game.
5. Venus Williams is a famous tennis player.
6. You can play tennis, too.

Simple Subjects and Predicates

- The **simple subject** is the main word in the subject part of a sentence. The simple subject is usually a noun or a pronoun.
- The **simple predicate** is the main word or words in the predicate. The simple predicate is a verb and any helping verbs it may have.

    EXAMPLE: My cousin keeps his car in the garage.

    Simple Subject — cousin
    Simple Predicate — keeps

A. Underline each subject. Then circle each simple subject within each subject.

1. The plans for a new car are made years ahead of time.

2. Many important decisions go into the design of a car.

3. Each part of the car is studied.

4. A clay model is made to show what the car will look like.

B. Underline each predicate. Then circle the simple predicate within each predicate.

1. Seven kinds of bears live in the world.

2. Most bears live in areas north of the equator.

3. Bears have small eyes.

4. Bears can live as long as thirty years.

5. A bear uses its claws to dig for food.

6. Brown bears usually eat grasses, berries, and nuts.

7. Seals and other animals are food for a polar bear.

8. Most bears sleep all winter.

9. Pandas are not really bears at all.

C. Write the simple subject and the simple predicate of each sentence.

1. The first basketball game was played in 1891.

   _____   _____

2. College teams played the sport in 1896.

   _____   _____

3. The first Olympic basketball game was in 1936.

   _____   _____

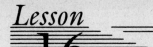

Lesson 16

Simple and Compound Sentences

> - A **simple sentence** has one subject and one predicate.
>   EXAMPLE: Fresh paint brightens a room.
> - A **compound sentence** is two simple sentences joined together by words such as and, but, so, and or.
>   EXAMPLE: I painted the den, **and** Kim painted the kitchen.

A. Write simple or compound before each sentence.

_____ **1.** We wanted to go camping, so we had to make plans.

_____ **2.** I voted for Yosemite, but Sam voted for the Grand Canyon.

_____ **3.** Sam got his way.

_____ **4.** Finally, the day to start arrived.

_____ **5.** I drove the camper, and Sam followed in the car.

_____ **6.** The scenery was wonderful.

_____ **7.** The canyon is almost too big to look real.

_____ **8.** We wanted to camp at the rim, but it was too crowded.

_____ **9.** We could sleep in the open, or we could use a tent.

_____ **10.** We decided to use a tent.

B. Make a compound sentence by adding a simple sentence to each group of words below.

1. Sleeping outside is fun, but

_____

2. The Grand Canyon is a great place to visit, and

_____

3. We could hike down the canyon, or

_____

4. Canyon burros look friendly, but

_____

Lesson 17

Combining Sentences

■ Short sentences about the same subject can often be **combined** into one sentence. Connecting words such as <u>and</u>, <u>but</u>, and <u>or</u> may be used to combine sentences.
  EXAMPLE: Sam went to the store. Joan went to the store, too. They went in a red car. **Combined sentence**—Sam and Joan went to the store in a red car.

A. Combine each pair of sentences.

1. We have to write a report. The report is on history.

_____

2. My subject is the Civil War. My subject is Robert E. Lee.

_____

3. We must use the encyclopedia. We must use other books.

_____

4. I should stop wasting time. I should start my report.

_____

B. Combine each set of sentences into one sentence.

1. Juan bought a horse. It is big. The horse is brown.

_____

2. The horse is kept in a barn. The barn is red. The barn is old.

_____

3. Juan rides the horse. Lynn rides the horse. They ride in a field.

_____

C. Write three short sentences about an animal. Then combine your sentences into one sentence.

_____

_____

_____

_____

■ A **run-on sentence** is two or more sentences that run together without correct punctuation. Correct a run-on sentence by making separate sentences from its parts.
   EXAMPLE: Many plants have seeds, the seeds grow into more plants, then those plants have seeds. **Correction**—Many plants have seeds. The seeds grow into more plants. Then those plants have seeds.

■ **Rewrite each story by separating each run-on sentence.**

One morning we found a baby bird it had been knocked from its nest by high winds its mother was nowhere to be seen. It was too young to fly, we took it inside to care for it. We were excited about taking care of the bird, we didn't know what to do about feeding it.

1. _____
2. _____
3. _____
4. _____
5. _____
6. _____
7. _____

The bird's little mouth flew open so often that we could not find enough insects to feed it. Then we found that the little bird liked dog food it also liked little bits of cooked egg yolk we even made some worms out of hamburger meat.

1. _____
2. _____
3. _____
4. _____

A. Write S on the line if the group of words is a sentence. Write X on the line if it is not a sentence.

_____ **1.** The first railroad passenger cars.

_____ **2.** The B & O offered the first rail passenger service.

_____ **3.** Passengers liked the speed of the train.

_____ **4.** Lots of savings in time and stress.

B. Write interrogative if the sentence is a question. If the sentence is a statement, rewrite it as a question.

1. Joseph flew to Boston. _____

2. Have you ever been to Boston? _____

3. Did you fly, or did you take the train? _____

4. Taking the train is slower. _____

C. Write imperative if the sentence is a command. Write exclamatory if the sentence shows surprise or emotion.

_____ **1.** Be more careful on this test.

_____ **2.** Take your time.

_____ **3.** Concentrate and read everything well.

_____ **4.** I can't believe it!

_____ **5.** My score was the highest in the class!

D. Draw one line under the subject and two lines under the predicate of each sentence. Then circle the simple subject and the simple predicate.

1. My cousin Lee plays hockey for the Hawks.

2. He practices early every morning.

3. Hockey players love the sport.

4. They play even in the coldest weather.

5. The game of hockey has very dedicated players and fans.

6. Players skate madly around the rink.

E. Write <u>simple</u> if the sentence is a simple sentence. Write <u>compound</u> if the sentence is a compound sentence.

_____ **1.** I went to the movies, and they stayed home.

_____ **2.** I think I had more fun.

_____ **3.** Then they decided to go to the same movie.

_____ **4.** I stayed home, and I still had more fun.

F. Rewrite the run-on sentence as shorter sentences.

Hank got up early he reviewed his notes again, so the test today would be easy for him.

_____

_____

G. Combine the sentences into a single sentence.

Andrea likes chicken. She likes chicken that is baked.

_____

H. Separate each run-on sentence in the paragraph below. Then write each sentence on a line.

I was tired of moving, my family had moved four times in the past three years. Leaving my friends was always the hardest it's not easy to start over and make new ones, now we can stay put in a town that I like.

1. _____

2. _____

3. _____

4. _____

5. _____

I. Write the type of sentence shown in parentheses on each line below.

(interrogatory) **1.** _____

(declarative) **2.** _____

(imperative) **3.** _____

(exclamatory) **4.** _____

A. Write <u>sentence</u> on the line if the group of words is a sentence.
If the group of words is not a sentence, rewrite it as a sentence.

1. Lee and Kenji are from Japan. _____

2. Three years ago, they. _____

3. Now they. _____

4. Lee and Kenji like their new home. _____

B. Underline the declarative sentences. Write the interrogative sentences.

How much do you know about the U.S. flag? The stripes on it stand for the first thirteen colonies. What do you think the stars stand for? The stars represent the fifty states. The colors have a meaning, too. White means freedom from wrong. Red stands for courage. Blue stands for fairness. Everything on the flag has a meaning. Did you know that?

1. _____

2. _____

3. _____

C. Rewrite the statements as questions.
1. Jetta ran to the grocery store.

_____

2. She bought bread and milk.

_____

3. She stopped at the park.

_____

4. Jetta was surprised at how long she was gone.

_____

D. Write one imperative sentence and one exclamatory sentence about an adventure.

1. _____

2. _____

E. Draw one line under the subject and two lines under the predicate of each sentence. Then write the simple subject and the simple predicate of each sentence.

Fingerprints can prove who a person is. A light powder is used so fingerprints can be seen. Each person's fingerprints are different from anyone else's fingerprints. Even the fingerprints of twins are different. A person's fingerprints stay the same as he or she grows older.

1. _____   _____

2. _____   _____

3. _____   _____

4. _____   _____

5. _____   _____

F. Underline the compound sentences. Write the simple sentences.

The main product of Florida is citrus fruit. Citrus fruit needs warm weather to grow. Oranges are grown in Florida, and grapefruit are also grown there. Other fruits grow in Florida, but citrus fruit is still the main crop. Many vegetables are also grown in Florida.

1. _____

2. _____

3. _____

G. Rewrite the paragraph. Combine short sentences and separate run-on sentences.

Flies are interesting insects. The eyes of a fly have up to 400 parts they really see only motion and light. A fly has six legs. Each fly has six feet. Each foot has a pair of claws.

_____

_____

_____

_____

_____

■ A **noun** is a word that names a person, place, or thing.
  EXAMPLES: person—woman, Anna; place—city, San Francisco;
  thing—dog, Fido

A. Underline the two nouns in each sentence.

1. Mrs. Smith has a big job ahead.
2. She needs to plan a picnic for her family.
3. Mrs. Smith must find a big park.
4. The family always enjoys the picnic.
5. It is a big event every year.
6. Mr. Smith is planning some games.
7. He will set up a net for volleyball.
8. Margie will make the hamburgers.
9. Mrs. Smith finally picked Riverview Park.
10. The park is on the Mississippi River.

B. Tell what each underlined noun is by writing person, place, or thing.

_____ 1. Buttons the dog

_____ 2. my brother John

_____ 3. the neighbor's uncle

_____ 4. 472 Elm Street

_____ 5. Orville's friend

_____ 6. Morris the cat

_____ 7. the city of Trenton

_____ 8. presented by the mayor

_____ 9. Sydney, Australia

_____ 10. my friend's sister

_____ 11. the state of Utah

_____ 12. a large cloud

_____ 13. a happy clown

Proper and Common Nouns

> - A **proper noun** names a particular person, place, or thing. It begins with a capital letter.
>   EXAMPLES: person—Mary; place—Dayton; thing—Queenie
> - A **common noun** does not name a particular person, place, or thing.
>   EXAMPLES: person—girl; place—city; thing—house

A. Underline the common nouns in each sentence.

1. My cousin Monica will visit for the holidays.

2. She loves Thanksgiving in the country.

3. My cousin is always a welcome visitor.

4. Her stories about New York are interesting.

5. This year, she is bringing Dr. Alvarado with her.

B. Underline the proper nouns in each sentence.

1. Dr. Alvarado is a doctor in New York.

2. She works at Parkside Hospital.

3. In September, she's going to teach a class in medicine.

4. The class will be at Roosevelt University in Queens, New York.

5. The students come from all over the United States.

C. Write a proper noun for each common noun given.

1. dog _____Spot_____

2. country _____

3. name _____

4. day _____

5. city _____

6. holiday _____

7. month _____

8. uncle _____

9. cat _____

10. friend _____

11. state _____

12. father _____

13. game _____

14. street _____

15. planet _____

16. school _____

17. teacher _____

18. continent _____

19. president _____

20. magazine _____

Singular and Plural Nouns

> - A **singular noun** names one person, place, or thing.
> - A **plural noun** names more than one person, place, or thing.
> - Add -s to most nouns to make them plural.
>   EXAMPLE: dog—dogs
> - Add -es to nouns ending in s, z, x, ch, or sh to make them plural.
>   EXAMPLES: dress—dresses, box—boxes
> - If a noun ends in a vowel and y, add -s to make it plural. If
>   the noun ends in a consonant and y, change the y to i and
>   add -es.
>   EXAMPLES: bay—bays, party—parties
> - If a noun ends with the f sound, change the f to v and add -es.
>   EXAMPLE: calf—calves
> - Sometimes the entire spelling is changed to form a plural noun.
>   EXAMPLES: child—children, goose—geese, mouse—mice

A. Write S before each singular noun below. Then write its plural form. Write P before each plural noun. Then write its singular form. You may wish to check the spellings in a dictionary.

_____ 1. porch _____

_____ 2. chair _____

_____ 3. girls _____

_____ 4. wife _____

_____ 5. flies _____

_____ 6. sky _____

_____ 7. foxes _____

_____ 8. halves _____

_____ 9. pencil _____

_____ 10. alley _____

_____ 11. leaves _____

_____ 12. pouch _____

_____ 13. inches _____

_____ 14. shelf _____

B. Circle the correct noun in parentheses. Write singular or plural on the lines.

_____ 1. After dinner we watch two (program, programs).

_____ 2. We limit our television viewing to one (hour, hours) a day.

_____ 3. The rest of the (time, times), we read or just chat about our day.

_____ 4. Our (family, families) has grown closer since we started this habit.

_____ 5. In fact, Lupe now prefers one of her (magazines, magazine) to TV.

_____ 6. I still like to watch a good (show, shows) now and then.

> - A **possessive noun** is a noun that tells who or what owns something.
> - Add an **apostrophe** (') and an -s to the end of most singular nouns to show that they are possessive nouns.
>   EXAMPLES: Tony's house, the dog's bone

A. Rewrite each of the phrases below using a possessive noun.

1. the house of my aunt   my aunt's house

2. the dog my cousin has

3. the books belonging to my friend

4. the bicycle of my brother

5. an apron belonging to the cook

B. Write the correct possessive form of the word in parentheses to complete each sentence.

1. (Jerry) _____ car was stolen.

2. The police (officer) _____ response was not encouraging.

3. He said the (thief) _____ trail was already cold.

4. He reported the (automobile) _____ last location.

5. Jerry hopes his (city) _____ police department will find it.

C. Write the correct possessive noun to complete the second sentence in each pair of sentences.

1. The store is having a sale. The _____ sale will last a week.

2. Lisa bought a coat. _____ coat has a heavy lining.

3. A clerk helped Lisa. The _____ job was to help people.

4. One shopping bag broke. The _____ contents spilled.

5. Another man helped her. Lisa was grateful for the

   _____ kindness.

Plural Possessive Nouns

> - A **plural possessive** noun shows ownership by more than one person or thing.
> - If a plural noun does not end in -s, the possessive is formed by adding an apostrophe and an -s (**'s**) to the noun.
>   EXAMPLE: men's teams
> - If a plural noun ends in -s, the possessive is usually formed by simply adding an apostrophe after the -s (**s'**).
>   EXAMPLE: birds' nests

A. **Write the correct plural possessive form of the word in parentheses to complete each sentence.**

1. My (sisters) _____ band is very popular.

2. The (uniforms) _____ colors are beautiful.

3. The band plays for (parents) _____ clubs.

4. The (members) _____ cheering was loud.

5. The (instruments) _____ sounds were perfect.

B. **Write the correct possessive noun to complete the second sentence in each pair of sentences.**

1. Fred and Carol are farmers. _____Farmers'_____ work can be very hard.

2. Their children help on the farm. Fred depends on the

   _____ help.

3. There are three ponds on the farm. The _____ water is very clear.

4. Fred keeps many sheep on his farm. He prepares the

   _____ food.

5. He gets milk from his cows. The _____ milking time is very early.

6. Three huge barns hold the animals. Painting the _____ walls is a hard job.

Lesson 24

Action Verbs

> ■ The **verb** is the main word in the predicate. If the verb tells an action that the subject is doing, it is called an **action verb.**
> EXAMPLES: Children **play** in the park. The squirrel **ran** up the tree.

A. Underline the action verb in each sentence.

1. Rex jumped at Tiger.
2. Tiger leaped for the tree.
3. Rex snapped back at the end of his rope.
4. Tiger quickly spun around.
5. Tiger arched her back.
6. Rex pulled against his rope.
7. Tiger danced sideways.
8. Rex howled loudly.
9. Then Tiger licked a furry paw.
10. She yawned slowly.
11. Rex chewed at the old rope.
12. He snarled at the cat.
13. Tiger teased Rex even more.
14. Rex pulled against the rope again.
15. Suddenly, it snapped.
16. Tiger shot into the air.
17. Rex bounded across the yard.
18. Tiger scrambled up the tree just in time.

B. Complete each sentence by adding a predicate with an action verb to each subject.

1. The captain of the team _____.

2. The coach _____.

3. All of the team members _____.

4. The fans _____.

5. The scorekeeper _____.

6. Everyone _____.

Linking Verbs

> ■ A **linking verb** does not show action. Instead, it links the subject to a word that either describes the subject or gives the subject another name. If a verb can be replaced by one of the verbs of being (<u>am</u>, <u>is</u>, <u>are</u>, <u>was</u>, <u>were</u>), then it is a linking verb.
>
> EXAMPLES: Football **is** exciting. (<u>Exciting</u> describes football.)
> They **were** a tired group. (<u>Group</u> is another name for <u>They</u>.)
> Yoko **grew** tired. (<u>Grew</u> can be replaced by <u>is</u> without changing the sentence.)

A. Complete each sentence with a different linking verb from the box.

are	feel	is	seem	sound
become	grow	look	smells	taste

1. Spring _____ a wonderful time of year.

2. The days _____ warm.

3. The air _____ fresh.

4. The flowers _____ pretty.

5. The evenings _____ lighter.

6. Spring vegetables _____ fresh.

7. The birds _____ cheerful.

8. We _____ more active.

B. Write <u>L</u> in front of each sentence that has a linking verb.

_____ 1. The day seemed dreary.

_____ 2. We decided to stay inside.

_____ 3. It was too cold and rainy outdoors.

_____ 4. Jenny started a roaring fire.

_____ 5. We were warm and cozy.

_____ 6. We felt comfortable.

Helping Verbs

> ■ A **helping verb** is sometimes used to help the main verb of a sentence. Helping verbs are often forms of the verb to be— am, is, are, was, were. The verbs has, have, and had are also used as helping verbs.   EXAMPLES: Jerry **has** gone to the store. I **am** watching for the bus.

■ **Circle the helping verb and underline the main verb in each sentence.**

1. For a long time, we had wanted to give Sherry a surprise party.

2. We had planned the party in the park the day before her birthday.

3. She has gone to the park almost every day.

4. We were waiting for her there.

5. Sherry was raking her yard.

6. We were looking around the park for her.

7. We couldn't find her.

8. We were forced to make other plans.

9. So Sherry was given her surprise party on her birthday.

10. Juana is going to the zoo today.

11. She has gone there once before.

12. Jack had told her to see the monkeys.

13. She was going last week.

14. She had planned a picnic.

15. I am going to the zoo with her.

16. I have seen the zoo before.

17. We are taking the bus.

18. Jack is meeting us there.

19. He is riding his bike.

20. We are looking forward to our zoo visit.

- The **tense** of a verb tells the time expressed by the verb.
  There are three tenses—present, past, and future.
- **Present tense** tells about what is happening now.
  EXAMPLE: I **am walking** my dog. I **walk** my dog.
- **Past tense** tells about something that happened before.
  EXAMPLE: I **walked** my dog yesterday.
- **Future tense** tells about something that will happen.
  EXAMPLE: I **will walk** my dog tonight.

A. Write present, past, or future to tell the tense of each underlined verb.

_____ 1. Jules Verne <u>wrote</u> about going to the moon.

_____ 2. Spaceships <u>were</u> still in the future.

_____ 3. Now we <u>can fly</u> to the moon.

_____ 4. A space shuttle <u>will lift</u> off tomorrow.

_____ 5. It <u>is stationed</u> in Florida.

_____ 6. The shuttle <u>helped</u> us explore space.

_____ 7. It <u>will help</u> us settle in space.

_____ 8. The shuttle <u>is taking</u> off now.

_____ 9. It <u>will return</u> in a week.

_____ 10. I <u>will go</u> to watch it land.

_____ 11. It <u>will be</u> a sight to remember.

**B. Complete each sentence by writing a verb in the tense shown
in parentheses.**

(past)   1. Joy _____ in the garden.

(present)   2. She _____ gardening.

(future)   3. The garden _____ many vegetables.

(present)   4. Joy _____ the garden to be nice.

(future)   5. She _____ flowers next week.

(past)   6. She _____ the garden last week.

Lesson 28

Regular Verbs

- The past tense of a **regular verb** is usually formed by adding -ed.
  EXAMPLE: jump—jumped
- If the word ends with a single consonant that has one vowel before it, double the final consonant and add -ed.
  EXAMPLE: skip—skipped
- If the word ends with a silent e, drop the e and add -ed.
  EXAMPLE: bake—baked
- If the root word ends in y, change the y to i and add -ed.
  EXAMPLE: worry—worried

A. Write the past tense of each verb to complete each sentence.

1. Ms. Willis (look) _____ out the window.

2. She (gasp) _____ at what she saw.

3. A hot-air balloon (settle) _____ onto her lawn.

4. Two men (step) _____ from the balloon.

5. Ms. Willis (hurry) _____ across the yard.

6. The balloon's basket (crush) _____ her flower bed.

7. One man (scratch) _____ his head in wonder.

8. He said they were (head) _____ for the fairgrounds.

9. The wind had (change) _____.

10. "We (drop) _____ in here instead," he said.

B. Rewrite each phrase in the past tense.

1. sail the boat

_____

2. steer a straight course

_____

3. carry the sail

_____

4. enjoy the fresh air and sunshine

_____

Lesson 29

Irregular Verbs

- Do not add -ed to form the past tense of **irregular verbs**. Change the spelling in a different way.   EXAMPLES:

Present	Past	Present	Past	Present	Past
begin	began	give	gave	say	said
break	broke	go	went	see	saw
choose	chose	grow	grew	sit	sat
come	came	know	knew	take	took
fall	fell	leave	left	throw	threw
fly	flew	run	ran	write	wrote

- **Complete each sentence by writing the past tense of the verb in parentheses.**

1. Monday I (go) _____ to a singing tryout.

2. I got up and (leave) _____ early.

3. I (take) _____ the address but couldn't find the building.

4. Finally, I (know) _____ I needed to ask for directions.

5. I (grow) _____ worried that I would miss my turn.

6. Then I (see) _____ a sign on a building.

7. It (give) _____ a list of the companies in the building.

8. I (sit) _____ on a bench for a few minutes to calm down.

9. I (come) _____ to the right place after all.

10. Then I (fly) _____ upstairs to the office.

11. A man at the front desk frowned and (say) _____ I was late.

12. He (begin) _____ by handing me a form.

13. I (write) _____ my name, address, and phone number.

14. Then the pencil lead (break) _____.

15. He took it from me and (throw) _____ it away.

16. I (choose) _____ another one from his desk.

17. On the way back to my chair, I slipped and (fall) _____.

18. The man (run) _____ to help me.

Making Subjects and Verbs Agree

- The **subject** and **verb** of a sentence must agree in number.
- A **singular** subject must have a singular verb.
- A **plural** subject must have a plural verb.
- You and I must have a plural verb.
    EXAMPLES: Mike **hits.** They **hit.** I **hit.** You **hit.**
- The singular form of a verb usually ends in -s or -es. Add -es to verbs that end in -s, -x, -z, -sh, and -ch.
    EXAMPLES: Juan **watches** the game. Amy **waxes** the car.

- Circle the verb that agrees with the subject of each sentence.
  Write <u>singular</u> or <u>plural</u> to show the number of the subject and verb.

1. Chickens (eat, eats) grain. _____plural_____

2. A chicken (lives, live) on the ground. _____

3. They (flies, fly) very little. _____

4. A farmer (feeds, feed) the chickens every day. _____

5. Chickens (scratches, scratch) the ground for food. _____

6. Forest fires (causes, cause) damage every year. _____

7. A forest fire (destroys, destroy) large areas. _____

8. People (fights, fight) a fire with water and chemicals. _____

9. A firebreak (slows, slow) down a fire. _____

10. A river (acts, act) as a firebreak. _____

11. Airplanes (drops, drop) water on forest fires. _____

12. A firefighter always (watches, watch) for danger. _____

13. High winds (spreads, spread) forest fires. _____

14. A forest fire (kills, kill) many trees. _____

15. Many animals (loses, lose) their homes. _____

16. A forest (need, needs) many seasons to recover. _____

17. Responsible people (helps, help) prevent forest fires. _____

- A **linking verb** is either singular or plural. The linking verb must match the subject of the sentence in number.
  EXAMPLES: Singular—The movie **is** shown twice daily.
  Plural—Both movies **are** shown twice daily.
- A linking verb can be in the present tense or past tense.
  EXAMPLES: Present tense—The movie **is** shown twice daily.
  Past tense—Both movies **were** shown twice daily.
- Use there is or there was with one person, place, or thing.
- Use there are or there were with more than one.
  EXAMPLES: There **is** a movie tonight. There **are** many movies showing at that theater.

A. Write am, is, are, was, or were to complete each sentence.

1. My cat _____ was _____ in the garden one day.

2. I _____ sure I saw her wiggle her whiskers.

3. Her whiskers _____ shorter when she was a kitten.

4. A whisker _____ an organ of touch.

5. Whiskers _____ important to a cat.

6. My cat's whiskers _____ very long.

7. Her fur _____ very long, too.

8. I think my cat _____ beautiful!

B. Write There is, There are, There was, or There were to complete each sentence.

1. _____ many kinds of horses.

2. _____ no horses in America at one time.

3. _____ a horse called the pinto that looks painted.

4. _____ many pintos that are famous.

5. _____ pinto horse clubs that you can join today.

6. _____ a national pinto horse club meeting every year.

7. _____ people working to save the pinto horse.

8. _____ a good reason for this—they are beautiful animals.

■ A **pronoun** is a word that takes the place of a noun.
■ A **subject pronoun** is used as the subject of a sentence or as part of the subject of a sentence. The subject pronouns are I, you, he, she, it, we, and they.
    EXAMPLES: **We** went to class. Shelly and **I** did homework together. **He** is going to help us.

A. Underline the subject pronoun in each sentence.

1. She rode her bike almost every day.
2. It was a beautiful mountain bike.
3. They go as fast as the wind.
4. You can go anywhere on a bike like that.
5. We wanted to ride the bike.
6. I asked for a ride.
7. He got to ride first.
8. Then I got to ride.

B. Complete each sentence by writing a subject pronoun to replace the word or words in parentheses. Pretend you are Bill.

1. Jeff and (Bill) _____I_____ left early for school.
2. (Jeff and I) _____ had a test to study for.
3. (Jeff) _____ had studied, but I hadn't.
4. (The test) _____ was on plants.
5. (Plants) _____ are important to study.
6. "Which part are (Bill) _____ studying?" Jeff asked.
7. (Mrs. Hobart) _____ says this is an important test.
8. (Bill) _____ am going to study hard.

C. Write three sentences of your own using subject pronouns.

1. _____
2. _____
3. _____

> ■ An **object pronoun** is used after an action verb or after words such as to, with, for, and by. The object pronouns are me, you, him, her, it, us, and them.   EXAMPLES: Jim told **him** to start. Alex bought the present for **her.**

A. Underline the object pronoun in each sentence.

1. Jeff won it in record time.

2. The speed of the run surprised us.

3. Jeff beat me by a mile.

4. Maria caught us in the last lap.

5. Wendy will give them the prize.

6. The speech will be made by you.

7. Then a special prize will be given to him.

8. Wendy told me the prize is a blue ribbon.

B. Complete each sentence by writing an object pronoun to replace the word or words in parentheses.

1. The teacher told (I) _____ to read my report.

2. I told (Mr. Sheen) _____ that the report wasn't ready.

3. Mr. Sheen asked when (the report) _____ would be finished.

4. He had warned (our class) _____ that the reports were due.

5. Some of (the reports) _____ were done.

6. A few students offered to read (their reports) _____.

7. The class listened to (Sonja) _____.

8. Mr. Sheen said he wanted (the reports) _____ all finished by Friday.

C. Write four sentences of your own using object pronouns.

1. _____

2. _____

3. _____

4. _____

- Remember that a pronoun is a word that takes the place of a noun.
- A subject pronoun is used as the subject of a sentence.
- An object pronoun is used after an action verb, or after words such as to, with, for, and by.
    EXAMPLE: **Sam** gave **the gift** to **the boys. He** gave **it** to **them.**

- **Choose the correct pronoun to replace the underlined nouns in each sentence. Then rewrite each sentence, using the pronoun. You may use a pronoun more than once.**

| He | she | It | him | her | They | them | We | us |

1. Luisa and I decided to attend the talk series at the library.

   _____

2. The talks would be every Wednesday evening for three weeks.

   _____

3. The first one was about the solar system.

   _____

4. We knew we would enjoy all of the talks.

   _____

5. Outer space has always been an interesting topic to Luisa and me.

   _____

6. The professor was an excellent speaker.

   _____

7. The audience listened closely to the speaker.

   _____

8. Luisa said the talk was one of the best Luisa had ever heard.

   _____

9. The new facts we learned surprised Luisa.

   _____

10. In fact, they surprised Luisa and me both.

   _____

> ■ A **possessive pronoun** is used to show who or what owns
> something. The possessive pronouns are <u>my</u>, <u>our</u>, <u>your</u>, <u>his</u>,
> <u>her</u>, <u>its</u>, and <u>their</u>.
>   EXAMPLES: Is this **your** coat? **His** cold is getting better.

■ **Complete each sentence by writing the correct possessive pronoun.**

1. _____ family and I were going camping.

2. Suddenly _____ car stalled in a dark forest.

3. _____ engine just would not run.

4. _____ family was stuck.

5. Richard almost lost _____ temper.

6. He didn't expect this from _____ car.

7. Julie spoke, and _____ voice made everyone quiet.

8. We held _____ tongues.

9. "_____ hands are trembling," Richard said to Julie.

10. "So are _____ hands," Julie answered.

11. "Look at the bears with _____ paws up in the air," said Julie.

12. Richard tried to start _____ car.

13. Julie held _____ breath while the bears looked at us.

14. The mother bear turned _____ cubs toward the woods.

15. _____ growls could be heard through the car windows.

16. We hid _____ heads below the windows.

17. One cub turned _____ head toward us.

18. I tried to get _____ camera out, but I couldn't.

19. _____ strap was caught on something.

20. "You can tell _____ friends about your adventure when

    we get back," said Richard.

Lesson 36

Adjectives

> ■ An **adjective** is a word that describes a noun. Adjectives tell
> **which one**, **what kind**, or **how many**.
> EXAMPLES: **happy** person, **brown** dog, **four** cars

A. Circle the two adjectives in each sentence.

1. The big cat chased the tiny mouse.
2. His sharp teeth flashed in the bright light.
3. The scared mouse ran through the small hole.
4. The speeding cat slipped on the wet floor.
5. The tired mouse hid in a dark corner.
6. The damp cat left in a big hurry.
7. The little mouse had a wide smile.

B. Add an adjective to each sentence in these paragraphs.

beautiful	green	Many	sparkling
fierce	dark	Gentle	Wild

_____ people go to the _____

national parks. They see _____ streams and

_____ forests. _____ animals roam

freely on _____ meadows. _____

deer and _____ bears both live in the forests.

bare	red	shaky	soft	thick
best	wooden	six	strong	young

The _____ man climbed the _____ ladder. A

_____ wind blew the _____ branches. His

_____ friend steadied the _____ ladder. He picked

_____ _____ apples. The _____ leaves

tickled his _____ arm.

Adjectives That Compare

> - Sometimes adjectives are used to compare one thing to another.
> - Most adjectives that compare two things end in -er.
>   EXAMPLE: The red chair is **bigger** than the blue chair.
> - Most adjectives that compare more than two things end in -est.
>   EXAMPLE: That chair is the **biggest** chair in the store.

A. Circle the correct adjective in each sentence.

1. Jean's puppy is the (smaller, smallest) of all the puppies.

2. He is (smaller, smallest) than his brother.

3. Toby was the (cuter, cutest) name Jean could think of.

4. Toby looked (funnier, funniest) than his sister.

5. He had the (whiter, whitest) fur of all the puppies.

6. Toby had the (longer, longest) ears Jean had ever seen.

7. Jean soon learned that Toby was the (naughtier, naughtiest) puppy she had ever known.

8. He played (harder, hardest) than his brother.

9. He stayed awake (later, latest) than his sister.

10. He kept Jean (busier, busiest) than the mother dog.

11. He was the (happier, happiest) puppy in the litter.

12. But he'll never be the (bigger, biggest) dog.

B. Add -er or -est to the end of each adjective to complete the sentences.

1. Tim's hair is light_____ than Jamie's.

2. Who has the dark_____ hair in class?

3. Ida has straight_____ hair than Tina.

4. Tina has the wild_____ hairdo of all.

5. Is her hair long_____ than Jamie's?

6. February is the short_____ month of the year.

7. January is long_____ than June.

8. July is warm_____ than February.

9. March is cold_____ than July.

10. Which do you think is the cold_____ month of all?

> - An **adverb** is a word that describes a verb. Adverbs tell
>   **how, when,** or **where.** Many adverbs end in -ly.
>   EXAMPLES: He ran **quickly.** She was sad **today.**
>   Water dripped **here yesterday.**

A. Circle the two adverbs in each sentence.

1. It was widely known that he would cheerfully fix anything.

2. Yesterday he was calmly asked to repair a faucet.

3. He quickly and loudly refused.

4. Later, he quietly apologized for his response.

B. Circle the adverb in each sentence. Then write how, when, or where to show what the adverb tells about the word it describes.

_____ 1. Jim walked quietly.

_____ 2. He sang softly as he walked.

_____ 3. Later, he ate lunch.

_____ 4. He sat there to eat.

C. Use adverbs from the list below to complete the sentences.

anxiously	quickly	Suddenly
brightly	quietly	there
hopelessly	slowly	totally

1. Sam ran _____ to the door.

2. He stood _____ for a minute.

3. _____, Sam ran out the door.

4. The sun shone _____.

5. He looked _____ over his shoulder.

6. He began to walk _____.

7. His quiet day was _____ ruined.

8. He tried _____ to make it to the party on time.

9. Finally, he knocked _____, then joined the party.

Adverbs That Compare

> - **Adverbs,** like adjectives, can be used to compare two or more things.
> - Most adverbs that compare two things end in -er.
>   EXAMPLE: I arrived **sooner** than you did.
> - Most adverbs that compare more than two things end in -est.
>   EXAMPLE: Ted runs the **fastest** of all the team members.
> - Sometimes more is used with a longer adverb when comparing two things. Sometimes most is used with a longer adverb when comparing more than two things.
>   EXAMPLES: I drove **more carefully** than John. Tim drove **most carefully** of all.

A. Circle the correct adverb in each sentence.

1. Jean worked (faster, fastest) than Debbie.

2. Debbie finished (later, latest) than Jean.

3. Of all the workers, Donna worked the (later, latest).

4. She wanted to be done (sooner, soonest) than Jean.

5. Debbie worked (more carefully, most carefully) of all.

6. No one tried (harder, hardest) than Debbie.

B. Complete each sentence by writing the correct form of each adverb in parentheses.

1. The swans arrived (late) _____ than the ducks.

2. Of all the birds, they flew the (quietly) _____.

3. The duck quacked (loudly) _____ than the swan.

4. The swan swam (peacefully) _____ than the duck.

5. The beautiful black swan swam the (near) _____ to me of all the birds.

6. He swam (slowly) _____ than the white swan.

7. I will be back here (soon) _____ than you.

8. The picture of the swans will be taken (carefully) _____ than my other picture.

Lesson 40
Using Words Correctly

> ■ **Good** is an adjective that describes nouns. **Well** is an adverb that tells how something is done.
> EXAMPLE: That is a **good** TV that works **well.**

A. Use good or well to complete each sentence.

1. George sings _____, and Jill is a _____ dancer.

2. They work _____ together.

3. Both George and Jill had _____ teachers.

4. They learned _____ from their teachers.

5. They perform their act _____.

6. Their piano music is very _____, too.

7. They both play the piano very _____.

8. Such _____ performers are hard to find.

9. Everyone who sees them perform has a _____ time.

10. I'm going to practice so that I can sing as _____ as George.

11. Don't you think that's a _____ idea?

> ■ Do not use a **no** word with another **no** word or after a contraction that ends with **-n't.** Some **no** words are **no, none, nobody, nothing, nowhere, never,** and **not.**
> EXAMPLES: Incorrect—**Nobody never** writes me letters.
> Correct—**Nobody ever** writes me letters.

B. Circle the correct word to complete each sentence.

1. The boy doesn't have (no, any) paper.

2. I haven't (no, any) extra paper for him to borrow.

3. The teacher has (nothing, anything) to give him, either.

4. Doesn't he (ever, never) bring extra paper?

5. Are you sure you don't have (no, any) paper?

6. Hasn't someone got (nothing, anything) to give him?

7. Why doesn't (anybody, nobody) ever plan ahead?

> ■ Those is an adjective used to describe a noun. Them is an object pronoun and is used after a verb or a word such as at, with, to, and for.
> EXAMPLES: I like **those** shoes. I'd like to buy **them**.

A. Write them or those to complete each sentence.

1. Did you see _____ boys?

2. I have not seen _____ this afternoon.

3. If I do see _____, I'll give _____ a speech.

4. Have you seen _____ models all over their room?

5. I told _____ to put _____ models away yesterday.

6. I'd better find _____ soon.

7. Otherwise, I might make _____ models disappear!

8. I am not happy with _____ boys at all!

> ■ Doesn't is singular. Use doesn't with one person, place, or thing.
> ■ Don't is plural. Use don't with more than one and with the words you and I.
> EXAMPLES: Ed **doesn't** have a ride home. We **don't** have room in the car.

B. Write doesn't or don't to complete each sentence.

1. Juan and Charles _____ want to miss the practice.

2. Charles _____ like to be late.

3. Juan thinks it _____ matter if they're late.

4. Jamie _____ seem to care if he goes to practice.

5. Juan and Charles _____ understand why he _____ want to go.

6. The coach _____ want anyone to miss a practice.

7. He says they can't win if they _____ practice.

8. I _____ doubt that for a minute.

A. Circle the common nouns in each sentence. Underline the proper nouns. Draw a box around the possessive nouns.

1. Mark took his old car.
2. He drove to the town of Chester.
3. Jan lives on a farm nearby.
4. He wanted to ride her horse, Bullet.
5. Bullet is Jan's favorite pet.
6. She has a horse, two dogs, and a burro.
7. The burro, All Ears, lives in the horse's barn.
8. The dogs' home is under the front porch.

B. Write **A**, **L**, or **H** to tell if the underlined verb is an action, linking, or helping verb.

_____ 1. Tony is packing tonight.

_____ 2. He leaves tomorrow.

_____ 3. Tony has always liked camping.

_____ 4. He seems happiest outdoors.

_____ 5. Tony was born in the city.

_____ 6. He grew used to walking everywhere.

_____ 7. Now he hikes outdoors for hours.

_____ 8. He carries with him everything he needs.

C. Complete each sentence by writing the underlined verb in the tense shown in parentheses.

(past)   1. Jeff receive _____ his diploma.

(future)   2. Now he decide _____ what to do next.

(present)   3. Will he choose _____ to get a job?

(past)   4. He go _____ into landscaping.

(present)   5. Jeff like _____ to plant things and watch them grow.

(past)   6. He grow _____ a wonderful garden for the city park.

D. Circle the verb that agrees with the subject of each sentence.

1. Recipes (is, are) directions for cooking.
2. (There is, There are) recipes for almost every type of food.
3. Some people (follow, follows) recipes each time they cook.
4. My grandmother rarely (use, used) one.
5. I always thought she (is, was) the best cook I ever knew.
6. (There was, There were) hundreds of recipes in her cookbook.
7. Her friends (was, were) always asking for her recipe for some dish.
8. She (give, gave) them her recipes, but not her cooking secrets.
9. Grandmother always (say, said) that only taste counted.
10. Recipes (is, are) fine to start with, but she always (add, added) something special.

E. Underline the pronouns in the sentences.

1. She gave him a book.
2. She bought it on sale.
3. Her favorite book is *Oliver Twist*.
4. He is reading it now and likes it.
5. She hoped he would be pleased.
6. They like to share their books.
7. She is finishing a mystery.
8. Then he will read it.
9. Science fiction books are his choice.
10. But she thinks he will like Sherlock Holmes, too.

F. Circle the adjective or adverb in each sentence. Then write adjective or adverb on the lines.

_____ 1. Julia Roberts is a movie actress.

_____ 2. Her dazzling smile makes others smile, too.

_____ 3. Some say she is a wonderful actress.

_____ 4. She is a bigger star than others her age.

_____ 5. Julia quickly rose to fame.

_____ 6. Later she dropped out of movies for a while.

_____ 7. She has tried harder than anyone to protect her privacy.

_____ 8. So far she has done a good job of it.

A. Read the paragraph. Then follow the directions.

As he stands outside the old house, Marty wonders if this is a good idea. He wants to go in, but the history of the house stops him. All of the people in Charleston know of Mr. Bremmer and this place. Marty starts to walk toward the door. He still wonders if he should.

1. List the nouns from the paragraph in the correct column.

Common	Proper
_____	_____
_____	_____
_____	_____
_____	
_____	

2. Rewrite the paragraph in the past tense.

_____

_____

_____

_____

_____

B. Circle the correct verb. Rewrite the sentences.

1. Some jobs (is, are) not worth the money.

_____

2. We (agree, agrees) with that.

_____

3. Whoever (watch, watches) this place must be brave.

_____

4. Marty (is, are) not sure that he (is, are) brave enough.

_____

C. Rewrite the paragraph. Replace the underlined nouns with pronouns.

Marty got up Marty's nerve and walked to the house.
The front of the house was dark. There were faces carved
in the stone. The faces looked mean. "The faces are
strange," Marty thought. The faces scared Marty. "Oh well,
here I go," Marty said to himself.

_____

_____

_____

_____

_____

D. Choose one adjective and one adverb to complete each sentence.

Adjectives		Adverbs	
noisy	scariest	barely	slowly
brighter	shaky	ever	strangely
rusty		quieter	

1. The _____ doorknob turned _____.

2. This was the _____ job he had _____ taken.

3. Except for the _____ doorknob, it was _____ than a library.

4. His _____ hand _____ touched the cobweb when he saw something awful.

5. Eyes _____ than fire were staring _____ from the corner.

E. Circle the correct words to complete the paragraph.

"This (don't, doesn't) look good," Marty
mumbled to himself. (Them, Those) eyes belong to
something. I (don't, doesn't) (never, ever) remember
seeing (nothing, anything) like those eyes before. If I
get out of here, I'll learn my lesson (good, well). You
won't (ever, never) find me in a place like this again."

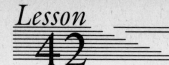
> - **Capitalize** the names of people and pets.
>   EXAMPLES: Laura Ingalls Wilder wrote many stories.
>   Did she have a lamb named Cotton?
> - Capitalize family names.
>   EXAMPLES: Uncle Bob married Aunt Margie.
>   Mom and Dad got married in California.

- **Rewrite these sentences using capital letters where needed.**

1. uncle george got up early today.

   _____

2. He and aunt beth had a special job to do.

   _____

3. uncle george and aunt beth were going to the animal shelter.

   _____

4. They wanted to find a puppy for susan and michael.

   _____

5. uncle george and aunt beth thought a small dog would be nice.

   _____

6. But susan and michael wanted a big dog.

   _____

7. uncle george saw a cute kitten named mittens.

   _____

8. In the very last cage, they saw sasha.

   _____

9. uncle george and aunt beth loved her at once.

   _____

10. When sasha ran circles around michael, he loved her, too.

   _____

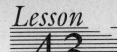

> ■ Capitalize each word in a place name.
>   EXAMPLES: Chicago, Germany, Utah, Howard School,
>   Main Library, Missouri River
> ■ Capitalize days of the week, months of the year, holidays,
>   and names of monuments.
>   EXAMPLES: Tuesday, February, Valentine's Day,
>   the Lincoln Memorial

A. Rewrite these sentences using capital letters where needed.

1. Our family will spend memorial day in washington.

   _____

2. We hope to see the white house and the washington monument.

   _____

3. We also want to see the smithsonian institution.

   _____

4. The potomac river forms a border between
   washington and virginia.

   _____

5. The lincoln memorial is amazing to see at night.

   _____

6. The vietnam memorial gets many visitors.

   _____

7. There are many amazing sights in washington.

   _____

B. Answer these questions. Use capital letters where needed.

1. When were you born?

   _____

2. What is your address? Include the city and state.

   _____

3. What is your favorite holiday?

   _____

■ Capitalize the first, last, and all important words in a book title. Words such as <u>a</u>, <u>an</u>, <u>and</u>, <u>but</u>, <u>by</u>, <u>for</u>, <u>in</u>, <u>of</u>, <u>on</u>, <u>from</u>, <u>the</u>, and <u>to</u> are not considered important words. They are not capitalized unless one of them is the first word in the title. Underline all titles of books.

    EXAMPLE: <u>A Present from Rosita</u>

■ Capitalize titles of respect.

    EXAMPLES: Major Thomas, Doctor Freeman

A. Rewrite these names and titles correctly. Underline the book titles.

1. doctor william h. black _____

2. judge rosa allen _____

3. The book: a wrinkle in time _____

4. captain william faircroft _____

5. The president of the united states _____

6. doctor laurie c. bell _____

7. The book: attack of the monster plants _____

8. major carol gates _____

9. The book: owls in the family _____

10. The book: my side of the mountain _____

B. Circle each letter that should be capitalized. Write the capital letter above it. Underline the book titles.

1. The results of mr. thomas's plan are interesting.

2. He wrote to judge george king and asked for his help in finding people to speak at our school.

3. judge king got judge claire booth to speak about her book, life in the courts.

4. So ms. dias told us to read life in the courts before judge booth spoke.

5. Another suggested book is a judge's story by raymond field.

Capitalizing Abbreviations

> - Capitalize **abbreviations** of days and months.
>   EXAMPLES: Sun., Mon., Tues., Wed., Thurs., Fri., Sat.
>   November—Nov., August—Aug.
> - Capitalize abbreviations for titles of respect.
>   EXAMPLES: Mr., Mrs., Dr.
> - Capitalize an **initial,** the first letter of a name.
>   EXAMPLE: T. J. Woodhouse

A. Write the correct abbreviation for the days and months of the year.

1. Tuesday _____

2. Wednesday _____

3. Thursday _____

4. Friday _____

5. Saturday _____

6. Sunday _____

7. January _____

8. November _____

9. September _____

10. August _____

11. October _____

12. December _____

B. Rewrite these sentences using capital letters where needed.

1. The conference is planned for aug. 12.

_____

2. It will be held in wm. Taft Park.

_____

3. George w. Bush will be there.

_____

4. Our mayor, ms. Foster, was pleased he could come.

_____

5. Police Chief e. s. Rodriguez will introduce him.

_____

6. Many people want to hear mr. Bush speak.

_____

7. They want to know how he likes life away from Washington, d. c.

_____

Capitalizing Parts of a Letter

- Capitalize the street name, city, and date in a letter. Also capitalize all letters in abbreviations for states. Together these words make up the **heading.**
    EXAMPLE: 1100 N. Main St.
                       Hartford, CT 06105
                       May 24, 1994
- Capitalize the **greeting.**
    EXAMPLE: Dear Mr. Jones,
- Capitalize the first word of the **closing.**
    EXAMPLES: Sincerely yours, Your friend,

■ **Underline the letters that should be capitalized in the letters.**

7216 melvin street
houston, tx 77040
october 23, 2006

dear fred,

  I am doing a report on farm life. Do you have any information you can send me? My report must be turned in three weeks from today. I can really use any help you can give me. Pictures and facts would be helpful. The names of some books I could find at the library would also help a lot.

your friend,
jesse

820 w. state st.
lockhart, al 36455
october 29, 2006

dear jesse,

  I'll be glad to help with your report. Better yet, why don't you come and visit? Call and let me know if you are coming. The library here serves all of alabama. I know we could find all the information you need.

your friend,
fred

Capitalizing and Punctuating Sentences

- Begin all sentences with a capital letter.
    EXAMPLE: Mary rode a bike.
- End a statement or a command with a **period. (.)**
    EXAMPLE: Jake rode a bike.
- End a question with a **question mark. (?)**
    EXAMPLE: Did Jake ride a bike?
- End an exclamation with an **exclamation point. (!)**
    EXAMPLE: Ouch, I fell!

A. Begin and end each sentence correctly. Put the correct punctuation mark at the end of each sentence, and circle any letters that should be capitalized.

1. i am going to ride my bike to the store
2. where is my bike
3. it is always in the garage by the hose
4. could it be on the back porch
5. i'll ask Joanne if she has seen it
6. she said it was in the garage this morning
7. oh, no, someone has stolen my bike
8. what should I do now
9. who could have taken it

B. Rewrite each sentence correctly.

1. i'll call the police about my bike

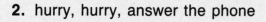

2. hurry, hurry, answer the phone

_____

3. hello, is this the police station

_____

4. yes, what can we do for you

_____

5. you must help me catch a bike thief

_____

6. how do you know your bike wasn't borrowed

_____

> - Use a **comma** (,) to take the place of the word <u>and</u> when three or more things are listed together in a sentence.
>   EXAMPLE: Mary, Pete, and George went to the beach.
> - Use a comma to separate the parts of a compound sentence.
>   EXAMPLE: Mary drove her car, but Peter walked.
> - Use a comma to set off words such as <u>yes</u>, <u>no</u>, and <u>well</u> at the beginning of a sentence.
>   EXAMPLE: Yes, I want to ride my bike.

- **Rewrite these sentences using commas correctly. Leave out the word <u>and</u> when possible.**

    1. I called Juan and Janet and Karen last Saturday.

    _____

    2. Yes they wanted to have a picnic.

    _____

    3. Juan packed a lunch and Karen brought a backpack.

    _____

    4. Well we were finally ready to go.

    _____

    5. Yes we found a perfect place by the beach.

    _____

    6. We played volleyball and swam and hiked.

    _____

    7. It was a great picnic and there were no ants around.

    _____

    8. We collected shells and driftwood and pebbles.

    _____

    9. Juan cleaned up the garbage and Karen packed the leftovers.

    _____

    10. We sang and laughed and read.

    _____

> - Use a comma to set off the name of a person spoken to.
>   EXAMPLE: Pam, you said we could go.
> - Use commas to set off a phrase that helps explain the subject of a sentence.
>   EXAMPLE: Mr. Gonzales, Rudy's father, is a lawyer.

A. Add commas where needed in each sentence.

1. Our neighbor Buddy Rush is gone.

2. Mr. Rush his father said he doesn't know where Buddy is.

3. Danny did Buddy talk about going somewhere?

4. This seems very strange to me Tim.

5. Chief Carter our sheriff thinks so, too.

6. Buddy where are you?

7. Danny don't you remember what I told you?

8. What should we do now Chief Carter?

B. Put an X in front of the sentence that tells about each numbered sentence.

1. Craig, your brother is here.

   _____ Craig is your brother.

   _____ Someone is talking to Craig.

2. Lydia, my friend will go, too.

   _____ Lydia is my friend.

   _____ Someone is talking to Lydia.

3. Our neighbor, Mrs. Hicks, is sick.

   _____ Mrs. Hicks is our neighbor.

   _____ Someone is talking to your neighbor.

4. Carrie, your sister is home.

   _____ Carrie is your sister.

   _____ Someone is talking to Carrie.

5. Anna, my dog, is loose.

   _____ Anna is my dog.

   _____ Someone is talking to Anna.

Lesson 50 — Using Commas in Letters

> ■ Use a comma between the city and state in the heading. Use a comma between the day and year.
>
> EXAMPLE: 872 Park Street
> Chicago, IL 60641
> September 17, 2006
>
> ■ Use a comma following the name in the greeting.
>
> EXAMPLES: Dear Nancy, Dear Mr. Muller,
>
> ■ Use a comma following the last word of the closing.
>
> EXAMPLES: Sincerely yours, Your friend,

A. Add commas where needed in the letters.

422 W. South St.

Dallas TX 72843

November 12, 2006

Dear Mark

Thank you for coming to my party. It was fun having you there. I also want to thank you for the great sweatshirt. It fits fine, and I really like it.

Your friend

Theresa

8200 Columbus Ave.

Dallas TX 72844

November 16, 2006

Dear Theresa

Don't forget about the trip to the museum on Saturday. See you there.

Sincerely

Mark

B. Add commas where they are needed in the headings.

1. 321 Pebble Beach Drive
   Jacksonville FL 32211
   November 17 2006

2. 101 Main St.
   Oakland CA 10032
   July 10 2006

C. Add commas where they are needed in the greetings and closings.

1. Dear Rosa

2. Sincerely yours

3. Your friend

4. Dear Grandmother

5. Your grandson

6. Hi, Scott

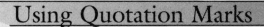

Using Quotation Marks

> ■ A **quote** tells the exact words someone says. Put **quotation marks** (" ") before and after the words. Use a comma, a period, a question mark, or an exclamation point between the quoted words and the rest of the sentence. Begin the first word of a direct quote with a capital letter.
>
> EXAMPLES: "Why don't you eat your cereal?" asked Jack. Jenny said, "I'm not hungry."

■ **Look at the pictures. See who is talking and what is being said. Tell what each speaker said. Include the word _said_ or _asked_ and the name of the speaker. Add quotation marks and commas where needed.**

Do you want to talk about the interesting places we each visited this summer?

Ms. Chen

My sister and I visited my aunt in Nome, Alaska.

James

We flew to Quebec to see our grandmother.

Jenny

We went to Arizona and saw the Grand Canyon.

Richard

1. What did Ms. Chen say?

"Do you want to talk about the interesting places we each visited this summer?" asked Ms. Chen.

2. What did James say?

_____

3. What did Jenny say?

_____

4. What did Richard say?

_____

More About Quotation Marks

> ■ Sometimes the speaker of a quote is named in the middle of the words being spoken. When this happens, quotation marks should be placed before and after both groups of words. Commas are placed inside the quotation marks at the end of the first group of words and again after the speaker's name.
> EXAMPLE: "I'd like to go," said Mary, "but I can't."

■ **Place quotation marks around the quotes. Add question marks and commas where needed.**

1. Well said Mike Dot is just getting over a strange accident.

2. What happened asked Susan.

3. A thought struck her said Mike.

4. Jake asked Why did you throw the alarm clock out the window

5. Because said Joan I wanted to see time fly.

6. What did one wall say to another asked Bonnie.

7. I'll meet you at the corner answered David.

8. What gets wetter Carlos asked the more you dry

9. A towel does said Angie.

10. Mother said Are your feet dirty

11. Yes replied Bobby but don't worry because I have my shoes on.

12. Maria asked How can you tell when an ice cube is nervous

13. It breaks out said Bill in a cold sweat.

14. Anna asked What is black-and-white and red all over

15. It's a blushing zebra said Jake.

16. What did the rug say to the floor asked Mike.

17. Don't move replied Bonnie because I've got you covered.

18. Joan asked Why do sponges do a good job

19. They become absorbed in their work said Carlos.

20. Angie asked Why is a pencil like a riddle

21. Because said Maria it's no good without a point.

Using Apostrophes in Contractions

- Use an **apostrophe** (') in a contraction to show where a letter or letters are taken out.
- <u>Won't</u> is an exception. will not = won't
- Contractions can be made by joining a verb and <u>not</u>.
  EXAMPLES: can not = can't, did not = didn't
- Contractions can also be made by joining a noun or pronoun and a verb.
  EXAMPLES: **It's** (it + is) a beautiful day.
  Susan's (Susan + is) going to the park.
  She'll (she + will) have a lot of fun.

A. Circle the correct meaning for the contraction in each sentence.

1. Donna said she'll go to the store today.   (she will, she had)

2. We're supposed to clean the house.   (We will, We are)

3. Beth and James say they'll clean the living room, too.
   (they will, they would)

4. I'll clean the kitchen.   (I would, I will)

5. She's going to be home soon.   (She is, She will)

6. We'd better get moving!   (We will, We had)

B. Write the contraction for the underlined words.

1. <u>It is</u> funny that <u>we are</u> lost.

   _____   _____

2. <u>You are</u> sure <u>we have</u> followed the directions correctly?

   _____   _____

3. <u>I am</u> sure <u>they will</u> start looking for us soon.

   _____   _____

4. We <u>did not</u> bring a map, but we <u>should have</u>.

   _____   _____

5. <u>I will</u> bet that <u>we will</u> be here all night.

   _____   _____

6. <u>We are</u> in trouble now because <u>I am</u> tired.

   _____   _____

> ■ Remember that apostrophes are not only used in contractions.
> They are also used to show ownership, or possession.
> EXAMPLES: Contraction—My **sister's** coming here.
> Possessive—My **sister's** friend is coming here. Both
> my **sisters'** friends are coming.

A. Rewrite each word in parentheses to show ownership. Use -'s or -s'.

1. Our family went on a picnic in my (brother) _____ car.

2. The (car) _____ windows would not go down.

3. (Dad) _____ clothes were soaked with sweat.

4. Both my (sisters) _____ jeans were wrinkled.

5. Finally my (family) _____ terrible trip was over.

6. We arrived at our (friends) _____ house for our picnic.

B. Rewrite each sentence. Replace each underlined phrase with a phrase that includes a possessive with an apostrophe.

1. We all liked the story Jennifer told the best.

_____

2. The setting of the story was an old castle.

_____

3. There was a prison in the basement of the castle.

_____

4. The attention of the students was on Jennifer as she read.

_____

5. A cruel man lived in the tower of the castle.

_____

6. The children of the cruel man weren't allowed to play.

_____

A. Circle the letters that need to be capitalized.

1. marjorie took her horse, blaze, out for a ride.
2. she rode through placeville to the miller house.
3. mr. miller's mother, judge miller, was on the supreme court.
4. judge miller served from sept. 1960 to aug. 1990.
5. her record was well-known in washington, d. c.
6. senator higgins often went to her for advice.
7. marjorie and her friends loved to hear judge miller talk about her experiences.

B. Put a period, a question mark, or an exclamation point on the blank following each sentence. Add commas where needed.

5780 W. Natchez
Miles VT 05857
December 10 2006

Dear Pam

It's been a long time since my last letter___ How are you___
Everything is fine here but I really miss having you as a neighbor___ Amy
our new neighbor is nice___ She goes to Taft School and she is in my
class___ No she will never replace you as my best friend___ Oh I almost
forgot___ Mrs. Tandy said "Tell Pam hello for me___" We all miss you
a lot___ Do you still think you can visit this summer___

Your friend
Delia

C. Add quotation marks, commas, and other punctuation marks where needed.

1. Henry stand by the door for a minute said Scott.
2. What for asked Henry.
3. I want you to hold the door answered Scott while I bring in this table.
4. Henry asked Are you going to carry that by yourself?
5. It's not very heavy said Scott.
6. What are you going to do with it asked Henry.
7. We need it for the kitchen said Scott.

D. Rewrite each sentence correctly.

1. well it's time to get to work said lisa

_____

2. lisa walked out of the room and jeremy followed her

_____

3. lisa pointed to the trash can

_____

4. what a mess jeremy cried

_____

5. your dog did this said lisa

_____

6. oh so now peanut's all mine said jeremy

_____

7. yes when he's bad he's yours said lisa

_____

8. they laughed and cleaned up the trash together

_____

E. Rewrite each sentence. Use apostrophes where needed.

1. Ill see what needs to be done with dinners leftovers.

_____

2. I think theyre cool enough to put on the refrigerators shelf.

_____

3. Dan hopes were not going to have that for tomorrows lunch.

_____

4. He doesnt think that his sisters daughters will eat it.

_____

5. Hes wrong; cold pizza is his nieces favorite food.

_____

6. Theyll be happy with this lunchs surprise.

_____

A. Circle letters that should be capitalized. Add needed commas, periods, exclamation points, quotation marks, and apostrophes.

miriam stone WBZIs top reporter woke up early. she said
I have plenty of time to get ready. she thought of the
letter she received yesterday:

> 920 s. lake st
> kansas city mo 43210
> april 1 2006
>
> dear miriam
>   if you want a really exciting story, meet me at the j m
> banister library at ten o'clock tomorrow morning. I m sure
> your stations newsroom will want this story.
>
>   yours truly
>   A Fan

she asked herself what it could be. miriam dressed ate
breakfast got her notebook and headed for the library. it was
not far and soon she was there.

suddenly a short woman in a dark dress walked up and
said I wrote the letter. she said you must hear my story.

my name is anna she said. Ive been tricked by a gang
of crooks. i need your help.

miriam said tell me your story and I'll see what I can do
anna told miriam of a man named general j c cook who
said he worked for the united states army. he told her he
needed a key to all the safety boxes in the bank where she
worked. yes she said it was strange but he said it was for
the country. now all of the boxes had been robbed and she
was sure it was general cooks work.

miriam was excited about the story. now said miriam tell
me everything you can remember about general j c cook.

wow what a story miriam said excitedly

B. Rewrite the letter. Add capital letters, periods, question marks, exclamation points, commas, quotation marks, and apostrophes where needed.

420 station st

park ridge il 60010

april 3 2006

dear mr thompson

i appreciate the time you spent with me tuesday ___ i learned a great deal about thompsons freight lines and i am sure that i would do a good job for your company ___ i have two years of experience in shipping goods around the world ___

it was a pleasure to meet you and speak with you ___ what a surprise to learn that you know my uncle joe so well ___ he speaks very highly of you and your company ___ thank you again for seeing me ___ ill call you in a few days ___

yours truly

wayne s carver

Writing Sentences

- Remember that a **sentence** is a group of words that tells a complete thought.
- A sentence must have at least two parts—a subject and a predicate.

      S   P
EXAMPLE: <u>Nora Vargas</u> <u>was bored</u>.

- **Read each group of words. Then answer the questions.**

1. Nora needed a hobby.

  a. Is there a subject? _____   If so, what is it? _____

  b. Is there a predicate? _____   If so, what is it? _____

  c. Is there a complete thought? _____   Is this a sentence? _____

2. Nora finally.

  a. Is there a subject? _____   If so, what is it? _____

  b. Is there a predicate? _____   If so, what is it? _____

  c. Is there a complete thought? _____   Is this a sentence? _____

3. Will do a family history.

  a. Is there a subject? _____   If so, what is it? _____

  b. Is there a predicate? _____   If so, what is it? _____

  c. Is there a complete thought? _____   Is this a sentence? _____

4. Nora began planning.

  a. Is there a subject? _____   If so, what is it? _____

  b. Is there a predicate? _____   If so, what is it? _____

  c. Is there a complete thought? _____   Is this a sentence? _____

5. Asked questions.

  a. Is there a subject? _____   If so, what is it? _____

  b. Is there a predicate? _____   If so, what is it? _____

  c. Is there a complete thought? _____   Is this a sentence? _____

> - A **paragraph** is a group of sentences about one main idea. There are usually several sentences in a paragraph. But sometimes a paragraph is only one sentence long. The first line of a paragraph is indented.
> - A **topic sentence** is a sentence that tells the main idea of a paragraph. The topic sentence is usually the first sentence in a paragraph.

A. Read the paragraph. Underline the topic sentence.

> Nora decided that she needed a hobby. She thought about different things to pick for a hobby. She thought about collecting coins or stamps. Nora finally chose to do a family history as her hobby.

B. Rewrite the sentences below in paragraph form. Put the topic sentence first and underline it. Remember to indent the first sentence.

1. To get the information she needed, Nora would have to ask many questions.
2. She thought about the kinds of questions she would ask.
3. She wanted to make sure that she didn't forget any questions.
4. So Nora wrote down a list of questions that she would ask each person.
5. Next she made copies of the list.
6. She put one person's name at the top of each copy.
7. Then she was ready to talk to people.

_____

_____

_____

_____

_____

_____

_____

> ■ Sentences with **supporting details** give more information about the main idea of a paragraph. Each sentence should contain details that support the topic sentence.

■ **Three sentences do not support the topic sentence. Draw a line through them. Then write the topic sentence and the five supporting sentences in paragraph form. Remember to indent the first sentence.**

Topic Sentence: Nora was ready to begin her history.

1. First, she put her questions into a notebook.
2. She made sure she had pens and extra paper.
3. Then Nora called Grandpa Casey and asked when she could come and talk to him.
4. She told Grandpa Casey about her new dog.
5. Grandpa Casey is fun.
6. She also called Grandpa Vargas.
7. Both of her grandfathers were glad to help with the family history.
8. Many of Nora's friends had hobbies.

_____

_____

_____

_____

_____

_____

_____

_____

_____

_____

_____

- **Time order** is used to tell things in the order in which they happened. Some words that help show time order are <u>first</u>, <u>next</u>, <u>then</u>, <u>afterward</u>, and <u>finally</u>.

■ **Number the sentences below in the order in which the events happened. Place the topic sentence first. Then write the sentences in paragraph form. Remember to indent the first sentence.**

_____ 1. He took a train from Canada to Boston.

_____ 2. He worked in Chicago for three years.

_____ 3. Casey came a long way on his journey to Sacramento.

_____ 4. First, he traveled by coach to Dublin, Ireland.

_____ 5. Finally, he left Chicago and drove to Sacramento.

_____ 6. After working for five years in Boston, he took a bus to Chicago.

_____ 7. Then he took a ship from Ireland to Canada.

_____ 8. He lived in Canada for two years.

_____ 9. He stayed in Dublin for only two months.

_____ 10. Now he enjoys telling about the cities he has lived in.

_____

_____

_____

_____

_____

_____

_____

_____

_____

_____

_____

_____

Writing a Conversation

> - When writing a **conversation,** be sure to:
>   - Use quotation marks around each quote.
>   - Use words such as <u>said</u> and <u>asked</u> with each quote.
>   - Begin a new paragraph for each quote.
>   EXAMPLES: Nora asked, "Will you tell me about your childhood?"
>   Grandpa said, "Of course I will."

- **Rewrite the paragraph as a conversation between Nora and Grandpa Vargas. Be sure to start a new paragraph for each quote.**

Nora asked Grandpa Vargas what it was like when he was growing up. Grandpa Vargas said he would tell her about his boyhood in Mexico. He said that his father raised sheep. He said that he used to watch the flock of sheep for his father. Grandpa said it was not an easy job because wolves were always nearby. Nora asked Grandpa Vargas to tell her about the wolves.

Nora asked, "What was it like when you were growing up?"

_____

_____

_____

_____

_____

_____

_____

_____

_____

_____

_____

_____

> - The **topic** is the subject you are writing about. The topic of a paragraph or story should be something that interests you.
> - The **audience** is the person or people who will read what you wrote. Before starting to write, ask yourself some questions: Who will read this? How old are the people who will read this? What kinds of things are they interested in?

A. Next to the list of topics, write <u>adult</u>, <u>teenager</u>, or <u>child</u> to show who might be most interested in the topic.

_____ 1. A story about the amount of gas different car models use

_____ 2. A picture book about baby animals

_____ 3. A story about dirt-bike racing

_____ 4. A travel story about Spain

_____ 5. Nursery rhymes

_____ 6. A story about a rock group's travels

_____ 7. A story about teenage movie stars

_____ 8. Fairy tales

_____ 9. The life story of a famous writer

_____ 10. A book of riddles

_____ 11. A book about home remodeling

B. Write five topics that are interesting. Then write the audience that you think might be interested in each topic.

Topic	Audience
1. _____	_____
2. _____	_____
3. _____	_____
4. _____	_____
5. _____	_____

- An **outline** is a plan to help organize writing. An outline lists the main ideas of a topic.
- An outline starts with a **statement** that tells the topic of the writing. The statement is followed by **main headings** and **subheadings** that tell what goes into each part. Main headings start with a roman numeral. Subheadings start with a capital letter.

Statement: Grandpa Vargas's life

(Main Heading)   I. Childhood

(Subheadings) {   A. Born in Mexico
      B. Moved to the U.S.

   II. Adult Years
      A. Worked in factory
      B. Started grocery store

- **Choose one of your topics from page 80. Write an outline for that topic. Use the sample outline as a guide.**

Statement: _____

I. _____

   A. _____

   B. _____

II. _____

   A. _____

   B. _____

III. _____

   A. _____

   B. _____

IV. _____

   A. _____

   B. _____

A Narrative Paragraph

> ■ A **narrative paragraph** tells a story. A narrative paragraph
> usually tells events in the order in which they happened.

■ **Read the model paragraph. Then follow the directions.**

"Ah," said Grandpa, "my meeting with the wolf was very exciting. We had just arrived at the meadow. This day, the sheep would not settle down. Blanco, my dog, was acting strangely, too. He kept circling the sheep, trying to keep them in a tight group. Suddenly, Blanco leaped on the back of one sheep and raced across the flock, back by back. Then, from a bunch of bushes, raced a huge gray form. 'Wolf!' my mind screamed, 'Wolf!' Blanco reached the edge of the flock just as the wolf did. Without slowing down, Blanco threw himself at the wolf. Next, I grabbed a stick and ran toward the wolf. I yelled and yelled and swung with the stick. I don't think I really ever touched the wolf. I was too scared to aim. Finally, I think he just got tired of all the noise we were making. He turned and trotted away. He didn't run, though. He made sure we knew that he wasn't afraid of us. Afterward, Blanco and I were very proud of ourselves."

1. Underline the topic sentence, and circle the time order words.

2. List the events of the story in the proper time order and in your own words.

   1. They had just arrived at the meadow. _____

_____

_____

_____

_____

_____

_____

_____

_____

Writing a Narrative Paragraph

To write a narrative paragraph, follow these steps:
- Choose a topic, or subject.
- Decide who your audience will be.
- Write a topic sentence.
- Add supporting details.
- Use time order words to help the reader know when the events happened.

■ **Choose a topic for a narrative paragraph. Write a topic sentence that will be the first sentence of your paragraph. Then add supporting sentences to complete the paragraph.**

Topic: _____

Topic Sentence: _____

_____

Paragraph:

_____

_____

_____

_____

_____

_____

_____

_____

_____

_____

_____

_____

_____

_____

A. Write sentence if the group of words is a sentence. If the group of words is not a sentence, add what you need to make it a sentence. Then write the completed sentence on the line.

1. Nora loved her grandfathers' stories.

   _____

2. Could listen for hours.

   _____

3. Their lives had been so exciting!

   _____

4. Wished her life was that interesting.

   _____

B. Read the paragraph. Underline the topic sentence.

      Nora wanted to make a lasting history of her family. She took notes while her grandfathers spoke. They talked very fast, so she missed some things. She decided to record the stories on tape next time.

C. Write the topic sentence and supporting details in paragraph form. One sentence does not support the topic sentence. Do not include it in your paragraph.

    Topic Sentence: Nora planned her recorded history.

1. She read through her list of questions.
2. Then she thought about how much time each would take to answer.
3. Next, she went shopping for blank tapes.
4. She also found a new shirt she wanted to buy.
5. Finally, she was ready to let her grandfathers tell their stories.

   _____

   _____

   _____

   _____

   _____

D. **Rewrite the paragraph as a conversation between Nora and Grandpa Casey.**

Nora asked Grandpa Casey how he came to the United States. Grandpa Casey told her of his trip from Ireland to Boston by ship. Nora asked him where his favorite place was. Grandpa Casey told her he liked it right where he was now.

_____

_____

_____

_____

E. **Write the following as an outline on the lines provided.**

Write a topic sentence   Write information about the topic
Choose a topic   Writing a narrative paragraph
Use time order words   Add supporting details

Statement: _____

I. _____

II. _____

III. _____

A. _____

B. _____

F. **Rewrite the sentences below in paragraph form. Write the topic sentence first. Circle the time order words.**

1. Grandpa's twin brothers played tricks on people.
2. First, they'd dress exactly alike.
3. Then they'd both answer when people said one of their names.
4. Finally, they'd look at each other and laugh.

_____

_____

_____

_____

A. Choose a topic about an event.

Topic: _____

B. Try to limit your topic to one statement that explains it.

Statement: _____

_____

C. Write a short outline about your topic listing the major points you want to include. You might want to include the time, the place, the people involved, the actual event, any comments made about the event, and your feelings about the event.

I. _____

   A. _____

   B. _____

II. _____

   A. _____

   B. _____

III. _____

   A. _____

   B. _____

   C. _____

IV. _____

   A. _____

   B. _____

V. _____

   A. _____

   B. _____

   C. _____

D. Write a topic sentence about your topic.

Topic Sentence: _____

_____

E. Write a narrative paragraph. Begin with your topic sentence. Refer to your outline for supporting sentences. Remember to indent the first sentence.

_____

_____

_____

_____

_____

_____

_____

_____

_____

_____

_____

_____

_____

_____

_____

_____

_____

_____

_____

- **Alphabetical order** is often used to organize names or words on a list. Use the first letter of each word to put the words in the order of the alphabet.
- If two words begin with the same letter, look at the second letter to see which would come first.   EXAMPLE: **f**a**n, **f**ine
- If the first and second letters are the same, look at the third letter.   EXAMPLE: **fi**ne, **fi**re

- **Read the groups of topics you have studied in this book. Number the terms in each group in alphabetical order.**

1. homonyms _____
   synonyms _____
   antonyms _____
   suffixes _____
   prefixes _____
   contractions _____
   vocabulary _____
   opposites _____

2. index _____
   accent _____
   pronunciation _____
   definitions _____
   alphabetical _____
   dictionaries _____
   respellings _____
   titles _____
   copyright _____

3. statements _____
   sentences _____
   commands _____
   subjects _____
   predicates _____
   exclamations _____
   questions _____
   run-ons _____

4. capitalization _____
   punctuation _____
   abbreviations _____
   initials _____
   quotes _____
   commas _____
   closing _____
   greeting _____
   periods _____

5. adjectives _____
   nouns _____
   verbs _____
   adverbs _____
   pronouns _____
   apostrophes _____
   possessives _____
   tenses _____

6. topics _____
   paragraphs _____
   details _____
   conversations _____
   sentences _____
   titles _____
   narrative _____
   audience _____
   outlines _____

> ■ **Guide words** are at the top of each page in a dictionary. Guide words tell the first and last words listed on each page. Every word listed on the page comes between the guide words.
>
> EXAMPLE: **million / modern:** The word <u>minute</u> will appear on the page. The word <u>music</u> will not.

A. Circle each word that would be on a page with these guide words.

1. alive / arrest	2. flame / fourth	3. settle / sink
anxious	fourth	side
amount	flower	shawl
accept	fog	seed
arrest	figure	seventeen
actor	fly	sink
alive	flame	service
also	fox	settle
adventure	flew	sign
ant	from	sleep
ashes	flight	shelter
allow	fruit	space

B. Rewrite each group of words in alphabetical order. Then write the words that would be the guide words for each group.

1. _____ / _____

lawn _____

last _____

lamp _____

late _____

lap _____

lake _____

lead _____

2. _____ / _____

palm _____

page _____

pass _____

pad _____

pack _____

pan _____

pat _____

Dictionary: Pronunciation

- Each word listed in a dictionary is followed by a respelling of the word. The respelling shows how to **pronounce,** or say, the word. The respelling is in parentheses following the entry word.
- **Accent marks** show which word parts are said with the most force.   EXAMPLE: freedom (frē′ dəm)   duty (do͞o′ tē)
- A **pronunciation key** (shown below) contains letters and special symbols, along with sample words, that show how the letters should be pronounced.

A. Write the word from the box for each respelling. Use the pronunciation key on the right.

gallop	hug	trout
girl	huge	vanish
glide	lowly	write

at; āpe; fär; câre; end; mē; it; īce; pîerce; hot; ōld, sông; fôrk; oil; out; up; ūse; rüle; pu̇ll; tûrn; chin; sing; shop; thin; **th**is; **hw** in **wh**ite; **zh** in treasure. The symbol ə stands for the unstressed vowel sound in about, taken, pencil, lemon, and circus.

1. (gûrl) _____

2. (lō′ lē) _____

3. (rīt) _____

4. (trout) _____

5. (glīd) _____

6. (hūj) _____

7. (gal′ əp) _____

8. (hug) _____

9. (van′ ish) _____

B. Complete each sentence. Write the word in the blank next to its respelling.

dictionary	found	guide	respelling	word

1. David didn't know how to say the (wûrd) _____ protection.

2. He took out his (dik′ shə ner′ ē) _____ .

3. He used (gīd) _____ words to find the page.

4. Then he (found) _____ the word.

5. The (rē spel′ ing) _____ was listed right after the word. He practiced saying it correctly.

Dictionary: Definitions

- The **definition,** or meaning, is given for each word listed in a dictionary. Sometimes a definition is followed by a sentence showing a use for the word.
- The **parts of speech** are also given for each word.
  EXAMPLE: **glove** (gluv) *n.* a covering for the hand: *I found a red glove on the bench at the park.*

A. Use the dictionary entries below to answer the questions.

folktale (fōk′ tāl′) *n.* a traditional story that has been handed down from generation to generation: *I am reading a book of folktales that I got from the library.*
follower (fol′ ō ər) *n.* someone who supports a person or a set of beliefs: *My friend is a follower of that senator.*
folly (fol′ ē) *n.* A lack of good sense: *It is folly to think you can go anywhere in this storm.*
fond (fond) *adj.* liking or loving: *I'm fond of my family.*
forbid (fər bid′) *v.* To order not to do something: *I forbid you to stay out after eight o'clock.*

n.	noun
pron.	pronoun
v.	verb
adj.	adjective
adv.	adverb
prep.	preposition

1. What part of speech is folktale? _____

2. What does adj. following the respelling of fond stand for? _____

3. What does v. following the respelling of forbid stand for? _____

4. Which words in the dictionary sample are nouns? _____

5. Write a sentence for the word folly. _____

_____

B. Use a dictionary to look up the meaning of each of the words below. Write a sentence for each word on the line.

1. griddle _____

_____

2. injury _____

_____

3. landlord _____

_____

4. pleasing _____

_____

> ■ Some words have more than one meaning, or **multiple meanings.** In the dictionary, the meanings for these words are numbered.
>
>   EXAMPLE: **hard** (härd) *adj.* **1.** very firm. **2.** difficult: *The letter was hard to read.*

A. Use the dictionary entries below to answer the questions.

barrier (bar′ ē ər) *n.* **1.** something that blocks progress or the way: *The deep river was an impossible barrier for the horseback riders to cross.* **2.** something that separates or divides: *Their age difference was a barrier.* **3.** something that hinders or limits: *His lack of good study habits was a barrier to higher grades.*

beam (bēm) *n.* **1.** a long piece of wood, iron, or steel ready to use in building. **2.** a ray of light: *The ship's beam shone through the fog.* **3.** a bright gleam or look: *The baby's smile was a beam of joy.*

bold (bōld) *adj.* **1.** having courage; fearless: *The first pilots were bold men.* **2.** impolite; rude: *The bold man cut in line.* **3.** standing out clearly: *The setting sun had bold orange colors.*

borrow (bôr′ ō) *v.* **1.** to get or take something with the understanding that it must be returned: *The library allows cardholders to borrow books for one month.* **2.** to take or use from another source and use as one's own; adopt: *Many words we use today are borrowed from foreign languages.*

by (bī) *prep.* **1.** next to; close to: *She sat by the window.* **2.** with the help or use of: *They came by the main road.* **3.** up to and beyond: *We drove by the gate.* **4.** in the period during: *He was used to working by night.* **5.** not later than: *Be home by nine.*

n.	noun
pron.	pronoun
v.	verb
adj.	adjective
adv.	adverb
prep.	preposition

1. How many definitions are listed for the word <u>barrier</u>? _____ for the word <u>beam</u>? _____ for the word <u>bold</u>? _____

2. How many definitions are given for the word <u>borrow</u>? _____ for the word <u>by</u>? _____

B. Write the number of the dictionary definition for the underlined word.

_____ 1. A <u>barrier</u> kept the fans off the playing field.

_____ 2. The mayor <u>borrowed</u> a joke from a friend to use in his speech.

_____ 3. Wooden <u>beams</u> were used to build the barn.

_____ 4. The <u>bold</u> captain led his ship through the hurricane.

_____ 5. They drove <u>by</u> the grocery store, but it was closed.

- An **encyclopedia** is a reference book that has articles on many different subjects. The articles are arranged in alphabetical order in different books, called **volumes.** Each volume is marked to show which subjects are inside.
- **Guide words** are used to show the first subject on each page.
- There is a listing of **cross-references** at the end of most articles to related subjects that the reader can use to get more information on that subject.

A. Read the sample encyclopedia entry below. Use it to answer the questions that follow.

VITAMINS are an important part of health. They cannot be produced by the body. Vitamins must be included in the diet. It is important to eat a variety of foods so your body will get all the vitamins it needs to stay healthy. Vitamins may be needed in increased amounts during periods of rapid growth, during stress, and while recovering from an illness. *See also* MINERALS.

1. What is the article about? _____

2. Why are vitamins important? _____

3. Why should you eat a variety of foods? _____

4. When might more vitamins be needed? _____

5. What other subject could you look at to get more information? _____

MINERALS are elements that serve as building blocks or take part in chemical processes in the body. Most of the mineral content of the body is in the bones. Calcium is an important mineral that aids in the formation of teeth and bones, blood clotting, and the activity of muscles and nerves. Minerals are found in foods.

6. Why do you think this cross-reference is included in the article about vitamins? _____

_____

7. Does the above cross-reference mention vitamins? _____

> - When looking for an article in the encyclopedia:
>   Always look up the last name of a person.
>   EXAMPLE: To find an article on Babe Ruth, look under <u>Ruth</u>.
>   Look up the first word in the name of a city, state, or country.
>   EXAMPLE: To find an article on New York City, look under
>   <u>New</u>. Look up the most important word in the name of a
>   general topic.
>   EXAMPLE: To find an article on the brown bear, look under
>   <u>bear</u>.

B. Write the word you would look under to find an article on each of the following subjects.

1. Nelson Mandela _____

2. frozen food _____

3. United States _____

4. oceans of the world _____

5. Margaret Thatcher _____

6. United Kingdom _____

7. children's games _____

8. breeds of dogs _____

C. The example below shows how the volumes of one encyclopedia are marked. The subjects are in alphabetical order. Write the number of the volume in which you would find each article.

A	B	C-CH	CI-CZ	D	E	F	G	H	I-J	K	L
1	2	3	4	5	6	7	8	9	10	11	12
M	N	O	P	Q-R	S	T	U-V	W-X-Y-Z	INDEX		
13	14	15	16	17	18	19	20	21	22		

_____ 1. caring for horses   _____ 5. mammals

_____ 2. life stages of the butterfly   _____ 6. Buckingham Palace

_____ 3. making paper   _____ 7. yeast

_____ 4. underwater plants   _____ 8. redwood trees

Parts of a Book

> - The **title page** tells the name of a book and the name of its author.
> - The **copyright page** tells who published the book, where it was published, and when it was published.
> - The **table of contents** lists the chapter or unit titles and the page numbers on which they begin. It is at the front of a book.
> - The **index** gives a detailed list of the topics in a book. It gives the page numbers for each topic. It is at the back of a book.

- **Use this book to answer the questions.**

  1. What is the title of this book?

     _____

  2. On what page does Unit Three start? _____

  3. List the pages that deal with apostrophes. _____

  4. What is the copyright date of this book? _____

  5. Who are the authors of this book?

     _____

  6. On what page is the lesson on prefixes? _____

  7. On what page does Unit Six start? _____

  8. On what page is the index? _____

  9. List the pages that deal with adverbs. _____

  10. What lesson is on page 42? _____

  11. On what pages are the lessons on action verbs? _____

  12. What company published this book?

     _____

  13. What lesson is on page 79?

     _____

A. Write the following words in alphabetical order.

fruit   onion _____   _____

morning   wag _____   _____

pizza   ran _____   _____

B. Write the words in alphabetical order under the correct guide words.

1. dear / delicious

_____

_____

_____

_____

2. delight / develop

_____

_____

_____

_____

depend
degree
debt
den
defend
demand
design
deck

C. Complete each sentence. Write the word in the blank next to its respelling.

1. If you (nēd) _____ help with a word, look in the dictionary.

2. The (dik′ shə ner′ ē) _____ tells you what a word means.

3. It also tells you how to (sā) _____ the word.

4. Often the word is used in a (sen′ təns) _____.

dictionary
need
say
sentence

D. Use the dictionary entries below to answer the questions.

chuck (chuk) *v.* **1.** to squeeze or pat with affection: *She chucked her son on the chin.* **2.** to toss or throw: *Dad chucked me the baseball.* **3.** to throw away: *The meat was bad, so I chucked it.*
ours (ourz) *pron.* that or those belonging to us: *Those books are ours.*

n.	noun
pron.	pronoun
v.	verb
adj.	adjective
adv.	adverb
prep.	preposition

1. What part of speech is the entry word <u>chuck</u>? _____

2. Which word is a pronoun? _____

3. Which word has more than one meaning? _____

E. Use the sample encyclopedia entry to answer the questions.

> **TWAIN,** MARK (1835–1910), was a writer whose works included many letters, books, and short stories. Most of his writing was humorous. He lived in Hannibal, Missouri, near the Mississippi River. Life there provided the backdrop for one of his best-known books, *The Adventures of Huckleberry Finn. See also* CLEMENS, SAMUEL L.

1. Who is the article about? _____

2. When did he die? _____

3. What is one of his most famous books? _____

4. Where did he live? _____

5. Why do you think the cross-reference is Samuel L. Clemens? _____

_____

F. The example below shows how the volumes of an encyclopedia are marked. Circle the word you would look under to find an article on each of the following. Then write the number of the volume in which you would find each article.

A–C	D–F	G–H	I–L	M–N	O–R	S–T	U–W	X–Z
1	2	3	4	5	6	7	8	9

_____ 1. the history of computers   _____ 4. animals of Norway

_____ 2. Albert Einstein   _____ 5. the capital of Romania

_____ 3. the Amazon River   _____ 6. bald eagles

G. Write title page, copyright page, table of contents, or index to tell where you would find this information.

1. The author's name _____

2. The title of the book _____

3. The page on which certain information can be found _____

4. The year the book was published _____

5. The page on which a certain chapter starts _____

6. The company that published the book _____

A. Use a social studies book to complete the exercise.

1. Find the title on the title page of the book.

   Write the title. _____

2. Find the name of the publisher and the year it was published.

   Write this information. _____

3. Find the names of the authors.

   Write the names. _____

4. How many sections or chapters are there in the book?

   Write the number. _____

5. Look carefully at the index.

   How are the words in the index listed? _____

6. Choose a person you have already studied this year in social studies.

   Write the person's name. _____

7. Look in the index for page numbers on which information about this person can be found.

   Write the page numbers. _____

8. In what chapter or chapters does the information about this person appear?

   Write the chapter numbers. _____

B. Look up the word <u>happiness</u> in a dictionary. Then follow the directions below.

1. Tell what part of speech <u>happiness</u> is. _____

2. Copy the first definition. _____

3. Write a sentence using the word <u>happiness</u>. _____

   _____

4. Copy the respelling. _____

C. Rewrite the words in alphabetical order. Then find the words in a dictionary. Next to each word, write the guide words from the top of the page and the respelling of the word.

| blizzard | scent | magician | howl | venture |
| helpful | remind | ache | ancient | disease |

	Words	Guide Words	Respelling
1.	ache	accuse / acorn	āk
2.	_____	_____	_____
3.	_____	_____	_____
4.	_____	_____	_____
5.	_____	_____	_____
6.	_____	_____	_____
7.	_____	_____	_____
8.	_____	_____	_____
9.	_____	_____	_____
10.	_____	_____	_____

D. Find the entry for <u>Chief Joseph</u> in an encyclopedia. Then answer the following questions.

1. What encyclopedia did you use? _____

2. When did Chief Joseph live? _____

3. Where did he die? _____

4. Why is Chief Joseph famous? _____

5. What Native American group did Chief Joseph lead? _____

6. Where did this group mainly live? _____

7. What kind of person was Chief Joseph? _____

Synonyms ▪ **Find the pair of synonyms in each sentence. Write each pair on the lines.**

1. Ruth smiled at Lea, and her friend grinned back.

   _____   _____

2. He ran out the door and dashed down the street.

   _____   _____

3. She spoke with Sarah, and then talked to her boss.

   _____   _____

Antonyms ▪ **For each underlined word, circle the correct antonym at the end of the sentence.**

1. He tried to find the <u>correct</u> answer. (write, wrong)
2. She <u>forgot</u> to pick up her clothes at the cleaners. (refused, remembered)
3. Miguel was <u>happy</u> to join the team. (pleased, sad)

Homonyms ▪ **Circle the correct homonym to complete each sentence.**

1. Joe and Jane did not (hear, here) the alarm.
2. They were (to, too, two) busy to notice it.
3. (Its, It's) hard to believe that, since the alarm is so loud.
4. I guess (there, their, they're) used to loud noises.
5. They were surprised to see (to, too, two) men run (right, write) past them.
6. The police got (there, their, they're) quickly.
7. They asked Joe and Jane to (right, write) down what they saw.
8. The police said about the alarm, "(Its, It's) purpose (hear, here) is to warn people."
9. Joe and Jane hung (there, their, they're) heads.
10. They were (to, too, two) embarrassed (to, too, two) say anything.

Multiple Meanings ▪ **Circle the correct meaning for each underlined word.**

1. Hank grabbed a rock to <u>arm</u> himself against the stray dog.

   part of the body   take up a weapon

2. The angry <u>bark</u> scared him.

   noise a dog makes   outside covering on a tree

3. Hank <u>dashed</u> for safety.

   drew a dotted line   ran quickly

Prefixes and Suffixes ▪ Write P if the underlined word has a prefix. Write S if it has a suffix.

_____ **1.** The thieves <u>disappeared</u>.

_____ **2.** One <u>rethought</u> what he had done.

_____ **3.** The <u>harmless</u> prank had gone wrong.

_____ **4.** He was <u>doubtful</u> anyone would understand.

_____ **5.** They could not <u>undo</u> what they had done.

Compound Words ▪ Underline the compound word in each sentence. Then write the two words that form each compound word on the lines.

1. My favorite dessert is strawberries and ice cream.

_____   _____

2. One of the most dangerous snakes is the rattlesnake.

_____   _____

3. He will use sandpaper to smooth the rough wood.

_____   _____

Contractions ▪ Write the contraction for each pair of words.

1. it is _____

2. could not _____

3. they will _____

4. I am _____

5. will not _____

Compound Words and Contractions ▪ Circle each compound word, and underline each contraction in the paragraph.

       Many people think he's gone to the seashore. But they're
wrong. He'd rather go to his mountaintop hideaway. He'll stay
there until somebody gets worried. Then they'll remember
and call him there. He won't let anything but an emergency
make him come back until he's ready!

**Recognizing Sentences ▪ Write S if the group of words is a sentence.
Write X if the group of words is not a sentence.**

_____ 1. Do you need?   _____ 5. If only.

_____ 2. Something from the store.   _____ 6. Will you go before noon?

_____ 3. I need milk and bread.   _____ 7. Then we can make lunch.

_____ 4. I'll get them for you.   _____ 8. Before Ellen and Jim return.

**Types of Sentences ▪ Write declarative, interrogative, imperative, or
exclamatory to show what type each sentence is.**

_____ 1. Do you have a ticket to the game?

_____ 2. No, I left mine at home!

_____ 3. Buy a new one.

_____ 4. Tickets cost three dollars.

_____ 5. Isn't it worth it?

_____ 6. Yes, I just don't have any money with me.

_____ 7. I will buy one for you.

_____ 8. Okay, let's go!

**Subjects and Predicates ▪ Write subject or predicate to show which part of each
sentence is underlined.**

_____ 1. Deserts receive the least amount of rainfall of any region.

_____ 2. Deserts have little or no plant life.

_____ 3. Some deserts are found near the equator.

_____ 4. Many desert regions have hot summers and cold winters.

**Simple Subjects and Predicates ▪ Circle the simple subject, and
underline the simple predicate in each sentence.**

1. For years factories dumped wastes into lakes and rivers.

2. Some waste materials cause no harm.

3. Other waste poisoned the water.

4. Today many factories protect the water from wastes.

Simple and Compound Sentences ▪ Write simple or compound before each sentence.

_____ 1. We know about all nine planets in our solar system, but we know most about Earth.

_____ 2. Earth travels around the sun.

_____ 3. Each planet follows a different path around the sun.

_____ 4. It takes about 365 days for Earth to travel around the sun, and we call this period of time one year.

_____ 5. Earth spins in its orbit around the sun.

_____ 6. The sun shines on different parts of Earth at different times, and this causes day and night.

Combining Sentences ▪ Combine each pair of simple sentences into a compound sentence.

1. Jessie went fishing. Ted went swimming.

_____

2. Yesterday was cold. Today is a rainy, gray day.

_____

3. Canada and the United States are neighbors. Canada and the United States are friends.

_____

Run-on Sentences ▪ Rewrite the story by separating each run-on sentence.

My grandmother was a pioneer, she traveled by wagon train to Missouri. When she turned 12, she decided she wanted to ride a horse, her father told her she couldn't do that in a skirt. So she had her mother make her some pants, she wanted to be on her own, she wanted more freedom. She kept a diary, I've read it all, that's how I know.

_____

_____

_____

_____

_____

_____

Nouns—Proper and Common ▪ Circle the common nouns, and underline the proper nouns.

1. Sally sat next to the window.

2. It was a wonderful morning in June.

3. Warm mornings in California are very beautiful.

Nouns — Singular, Plural, and Possessive ▪ Circle the correct form of each noun.

1. Our female (dog, dog's) puppies are brown and white.

2. All the (puppy's, puppies') ears are long.

3. Our other (dogs, dog's) stay away from the puppies.

4. The puppies' (tail's, tails) wag all the time.

Verbs—Action, Linking, and Helping ▪ Write A, L, or H to tell if the underlined verb is an action, linking, or helping verb.

_____ 1. The storm <u>blew</u> in quickly.

_____ 2. We <u>felt</u> the weather change.

_____ 3. We <u>are</u> going back to the house.

_____ 4. Then lightning <u>split</u> the sky.

_____ 5. Rain <u>was</u> predicted.

_____ 6. The storm <u>is</u> very strong.

Verb Tenses ▪ Write <u>past</u>, <u>present</u>, or <u>future</u> for each underlined verb.

_____ 1. Most hurricanes <u>form</u> in the spring.

_____ 2. We hope the next hurricane <u>will</u> not <u>hit</u> the coast.

_____ 3. The last hurricane <u>slammed</u> into Florida.

Verbs—Making Subjects and Verbs Agree ▪ Circle the verb in each sentence. Then write <u>singular</u> or <u>plural</u> to show the number of the subject and verb.

_____ 1. There are people who check facts for a living.

_____ 2. They read articles to be sure the truth is told.

_____ 3. Henry is one of those people.

_____ 4. He likes his job very much.

Pronouns ▪ Rewrite each sentence using the correct pronoun for the underlined noun. Then label each pronoun, using <u>S</u> for subject, <u>O</u> for object, or <u>P</u> for possessive.

_____ 1. <u>Carol's</u> job is park ranger.

_____

_____ 2. <u>Carol</u> loves spending every day in the forest.

_____

_____ 3. Her favorite thing is walking among <u>the trees</u>.

_____

_____ 4. She really likes it when <u>the trees'</u> leaves change.

_____

_____ 5. Ed sometimes brings <u>Ed's</u> camera to take pictures.

_____

_____ 6. <u>The camera's</u> pictures are clear and sharp.

_____

Adjectives and Adverbs ▪ Write <u>adjective</u> or <u>adverb</u> for each underlined word.

_____ 1. Terri walked <u>slowly</u> into the room.

_____ 2. Her <u>bright</u> jacket seemed out of place.

_____ 3. Her <u>shaky</u> voice showed how scared she was.

_____ 4. Her eyes looked <u>larger</u> than normal.

_____ 5. <u>Soon</u> she began to calm down.

_____ 6. <u>Finally,</u> she spoke with confidence.

Using Words Correctly ▪ Circle the correct word to complete each sentence.

1. I (doesn't, don't) want to be late for the meeting.
2. Nobody (never, ever) remembers exactly what happened.
3. I like to take (good, well) notes.
4. Then I can review (those, them) later.
5. It (doesn't, don't) take long to get there.
6. I just need to find (them, those) directions.
7. Everything will turn out (good, well).

Capitalization and Punctuation ▪ Rewrite the letter below. Add capital letters, periods, commas, question marks, and quotation marks where needed.

328 n state st
new york ny 10010
january 2 2006

dear dr turner

I want to thank you for your kindness to tootsie my pet bird my friend Jack said, no one knows how to cure birds they're different from other types of pets you shouldn't waste your money can you believe that I didn't agree with Jack so I brought tootsie to your office thanks to you, tootsie is fine again

sincerely
carlos gomez

Capitalization and Punctuation ▪ Rewrite each sentence correctly.

1. our next topic said mr lopez will be the fall of the roman empire

   _____

2. hurry and get out of there cried louis

   _____

3. ted please don't ask me to do that

   _____

4. has the jury reached a verdict asked judge mallory

   _____

5. eric said i'll be the first to tell you if you're right

   _____

6. well i guess it's all right

   _____

7. we spent the day swimming hiking and having a picnic

   _____

Using Apostrophes ▪ Rewrite the sentences. Insert apostrophes where they are needed.

1. Didnt you see the look on Deans face?

   _____

2. Its pretty clear he doesnt like our plan.

   _____

3. He hasnt said anything at all about Franks idea.

   _____

4. Were going to have to make up our minds soon.

   _____

5. The mens ideas are different from ours.

   _____

6. Everyones ideas should be considered.

   _____

Topic Sentences and Supporting Details ▪ Underline the topic sentence. Draw a line through details that do not support the topic sentence. Then circle the time order words. Rewrite the remaining sentences on the lines below.

Forests grow in a cycle. There are many kinds of animals in a forest. First, the strongest trees grow very large. Then the other trees cannot get enough sunlight. Weaker trees either stay short or die. Afterward, new growth begins. Sometimes fires destroy a whole forest.

_____

_____

_____

_____

_____

Writing a Conversation ▪ Rewrite the paragraph as a conversation between Chris and Bob.

Bob asked Chris if he understood the movie. Chris said he wasn't sure. He thought he had at first, but then he became confused. Bob agreed. Chris asked Bob what he thought about the movie. Bob said he liked it, but he wondered about the ending. Chris said the person who wrote it was probably as confused as they were!

_____

_____

_____

_____

_____

_____

_____

_____

Planning an Outline ▪ **Write the following as an outline on the lines provided.**

Clothing
Saddle and bridle
Cowboys in the Old West
Equipment
Gun and rope

Statement: _____

I. _____

    A. _____

    B. _____

II. _____

A Narrative Paragraph ▪ **Rewrite the paragraph in the correct order.**

      Judy had planned her day well. After that, she went shopping for a special meal. Tonight she would invite her parents over for dinner. Then she bought a beautiful bunch of flowers. First, she cleaned her entire house. She chose the clothes she would wear. Next, she went to the florist and bought a blue glass vase. She took the vase and flowers back home and put them on the table. Finally, she prepared the meal and waited for her parents to arrive.

_____

_____

_____

_____

_____

_____

_____

_____

_____

_____

Alphabetical Order and Guide Words ▪ Rewrite each list in alphabetical order. Then write the words that would be the guide words for each list.

Guide Words	Guide Words
_____ / _____	_____ / _____

1. right _____
2. rock _____
3. rich _____
4. rinse _____
5. rob _____

1. bat _____
2. back _____
3. ball _____
4. base _____
5. baby _____

Pronunciation ▪ Use a dictionary to find each word listed. Write the respelling of each word.

1. now _____
2. later _____
3. tomorrow _____
4. today _____
5. direct _____
6. scissors _____

Dictionary Definitions ▪ Use the dictionary entry below to answer the questions.

> **better** (bet′ ər) *adj.* **1.** higher in quality: *Diamonds are the better gem.*
> **2.** more satisfactory, useful, or desirable: *She got a better grade than I did.*
> **3.** more healthy than before: *He is better today.*—*v.* **1.** to improve: *She
> bettered her home life.* **2.** to exceed: *He bettered his score.*

n.	noun
pron.	pronoun
v.	verb
adj.	adjective
adv.	adverb
prep.	preposition

1. What does adj. stand for? _____

2. How many definitions for better are given? _____

3. What two parts of speech can better be? _____

4. Which part of speech and definition number are used for better in these sentences?

   a. She has bettered her tennis form. _____

   b. That horse is the better cow pony. _____

   c. He has a better car than his father has. _____

Using an Encyclopedia ▪ Read the sample encyclopedia entry below. Use it to answer the questions that follow.

> **ELBOW** The elbow is a joint between the upper and lower arm. This joint allows the arm to bend, twist, and turn. Groups of muscles and tendons make the elbow work. One of the best tools the body has is the arm. It allows a person to reach out, hold, and control things. *See also* ARM *and* WRIST.

1. What is the article about? _____

2. What is the elbow? _____

3. Why is the elbow important? _____

4. What are the cross-references? _____

5. Are both cross-references mentioned in the article? _____

Using an Encyclopedia ▪ Circle the word you would look under to find an article on each of the following. Then write the number of the volume in which you would find it.

A–C	D–F	G–I	J–L	M–N	O–Q	R–S	T–V	W–Z
1	2	3	4	5	6	7	8	9

_____ 1. the sea floor

_____ 2. Hong Kong

_____ 3. nursing skills

_____ 4. the life cycle of the fly

_____ 5. Helen Keller

_____ 6. how aluminum is made

_____ 7. the truth about vampires

_____ 8. breeds of horses

_____ 9. the plays of Shakespeare

_____ 10. boomerangs as weapons

_____ 11. string instruments

_____ 12. New Orleans

Parts of a Book ▪ Write title page, copyright page, table of contents, or index to tell where you would find this information.

1. a chapter title _____

2. the page on which certain information can be found _____

3. the author's name _____

4. the year the book was published _____

A. Write <u>S</u> before each pair of synonyms, <u>A</u> before each pair of antonyms, and <u>H</u> before each pair of homonyms.

_____ **1.** there, their   _____ **3.** deep, shallow

_____ **2.** tiny, small   _____ **4.** push, shove

B. Circle the correct definition for the underlined word in the sentence.

1. He is a good <u>pupil</u>.

part of the eye   a student

C. Write <u>P</u> before each word with a prefix, <u>S</u> before each word with a suffix, and <u>C</u> before each compound word.

_____ **1.** warehouse   _____ **3.** hopeful

_____ **2.** undone   _____ **4.** friendly

D. Write a contraction for the underlined words.

_____ **1.** I would go   _____ **2.** They will stay.

E. Write <u>D</u> before the declarative sentence, <u>IM</u> before the imperative sentence, <u>E</u> before the exclamatory sentence, and <u>IN</u> before the interrogative sentence.

_____ **1.** Where are you going?   _____ **3.** Go back.

_____ **2.** No, I can't!   _____ **4.** She stayed in the house.

F. Draw a line between the subject and the predicate. Underline the simple subject once and the simple predicate twice.

1. He asked me a question.   **2.** I did not have an answer.

G. Combine the sentences into one sentence.

I watched television. It was a new show.

_____

H. Separate the run-on sentence.

The wind blew over the trash can, I cleaned up the mess.

_____

I. Underline the common nouns, and circle the proper nouns in the sentence.

The photographs of Mary in the show were some of Rick's best.

J. Write the correct possessive noun to complete the sentence.

The children bought candy. The _____ candy was sticky.

K. Write **A** if the underlined verb is an action verb, **L** if it is a linking verb, and **H** if it is a helping verb.

_____ **1.** The thunder <u>sounds</u> angry.

_____ **2.** Edgar <u>kicked</u> it back in place.

_____ **3.** She <u>had</u> waited for a long time.

L. Write <u>past</u>, <u>present</u>, or <u>future</u> to show the tense of each underlined verb.

_____ **1.** James <u>is turning</u> around.

_____ **2.** He <u>will see</u> what we have done.

_____ **3.** But Eric <u>was</u> too fast.

M. Circle the correct verb in each sentence.

1. Plants (grow, growing) in the sun.   **2.** A healthy plant (need, needs) much care.

N. Complete each sentence by writing the correct pronoun for the words in parentheses.

1. The actors really knew (the actors') _____ lines.

2. The play was the best (Jill and I) _____ had ever seen.

O. In the sentence below, underline each adjective, and circle each adverb.

Yesterday I stepped carefully around the sleeping dog.

P. Circle the correct word to complete each sentence.

1. The coat fits her (good, well).

2. (Don't, Doesn't) you have (no, any) gloves that match?

Q. In the letter below, underline letters that should be capitalized, and add punctuation where needed.

707 s baywood st

sacramento ca 90034

feb 10 2006

dear sally

   when are you and dave coming for a visit ___ I cant wait to show you my new house ___ the neighborhoods got everything i need ___ i really love it here ___

                    your friend

                    todd

R. Rewrite the sentences below in paragraph form. Put the topic sentence first, and circle the time order words.

1. Then I planted the seeds.
2. I decided to raise a vegetable garden.
3. First, I prepared the soil.
4. Finally, I watered the seeds.

_____

_____

_____

_____

S. Using the words and phrases below, fill in the outline.

Prepare the soil   Raising a vegetable garden

Planting   Plant and water the seeds

Statement: _____

      I. _____

          A. _____

          B. _____

T. Use the dictionary entry below to answer the questions.

cotton (kŏt′ n) *n.* **1.** plant or shrub grown for its fibers: *Cotton is our main crop.* **2.** the soft, white fiber around cotton seeds, used for making cloth and thread: *She wove the cotton into cloth.* **3.** cloth or thread made of cotton: *His shirt is made of cotton.*

n.	noun
pron.	pronoun
v.	verb
adj.	adjective
adv.	adverb
prep.	preposition

1. What part of speech is the word <u>cotton</u>? _____

2. Would <u>cork</u> or <u>could</u> come before <u>cotton</u> in the dictionary?

_____

3. Would <u>cost</u> / <u>cot</u> or <u>corn</u> / <u>couch</u> be the guide words for <u>cotton</u>?

_____

U. Use the sample encyclopedia entry to answer the questions.

DEPRESSION, THE GREAT (1929–1938). The Great Depression was a time in history when the economy in the United States was very bad. Many people faced starvation and lost their homes. *See also* HERBERT HOOVER.

1. What is this article about? _____

2. What is the cross-reference? _____

_____

Below is a list of the sections on *Check What You've Learned* and the pages on which the skills in each section are taught. If you missed any questions, turn to the pages listed, and practice the skills. Then correct the problems you missed on *Check What You've Learned.*

Check What You Know (P. 1)

A. 1. A
2. H
3. S
4. S

B. 1. sound made with fingers

C. 1. S
2. P
3. C
4. P

D. 1. won't
2. I'm

E. 1. E, That is a great shirt!
2. IN, Can't you see that it's too big?
3. D, I think it fits just fine.
4. IM, (You) Take it back to the store.

F. 1. It / is raining outside.
2. There / are puddles in the street.

G. Sentences may vary. Suggested:
Jerry went out to dinner at the new restaurant.

H. Alex cooked a big meal. He served it to his friends.

Check What You Know (P. 2)

I. The words in bold should be circled.
Betty chose two dogs, **Yip** and **Yap**, to take home to her children.

J. mailbox's

K. 1. A
2. L
3. H

L. 1. future
2. past
3. present

M. 1. is
2. come

N. 1. we
2. them

O. The words in bold should be circled.
We **carefully** planned an exciting surprise party for Henry.

P. 1. ever
2. Those, don't

Check What You Know (P. 3)

Q.   977 N. Seaside Dr.
Ann Arbor, MI 68445
Jan. 25, 2006

Dear Kathleen,
  Mario and I took Ginger to the vet to get her shots. She really hates to go!
  How is Frisky? I hope you are both fine.
                Your friend,
                Elena

R. The words in bold should be circled.
  We just moved into a new house.
First, the dog next door began barking all night. **Then** we spoke to the neighbors.
Finally, we had peace and quiet.

S. Statement: Taking a phone message
 I. Information needed from caller
   A. Name and number
   B. Message

Check What You Know (P. 4)

T. 1. adjective
2. baby
3. bacon / bake

U. 1. John James Audubon
2. Audubon Society

Unit 1 Vocabulary

Lesson 1, Synonyms (P. 5)

A.
1. desire
2. outdoors
3. seeing
4. write
5. match
6. ask
7. ideas
8. little
9. enjoy
10. grew
11. arranged

B.
1. The <u>common</u> hive has many worker bees.
2. It is not <u>uncommon</u> to find 80,000 <u>active</u> workers in a colony.
3. The <u>brave</u> worker bee will do anything to <u>halt</u> the enemies of the hive.
4. The hive must <u>stay</u> warm, or the bees will die.
5. Farmers are <u>glad</u> to see <u>large</u> hives near their fields.

Lesson 2, Antonyms (P. 6)

A.
1. sharp
2. soft
3. wrong
4. save
5. forget
6. messy
7. begin
8. new
9. top

B. Answers will vary. Suggested antonyms: big, clean, good, cleaned, brighten, drying, wrong, same

Lesson 3, Homonyms (P. 7)

A.
1. its
2. it's
3. it's
4. it's
5. its
6. its
7. it's
8. its
9. it's

B.
1. There
2. They're
3. they're
4. their
5. there
6. Their
7. they're
8. their

Lesson 4, More Homonyms (P. 8)

A.
1. two, to
2. too, to
3. to
4. two

B.
1. write
2. right
3. right
4. right

C.
1. hear
2. here, hear
3. here, hear
4. here

Lesson 5, Multiple Meanings (P. 9)

A.
1. pillow
2. salty liquid from the eye
3. strike over and over
4. make the sound of a bell
5. loud noise
6. heavy winds with rain or snow
7. guide

B. Discuss your answers with your instructor.

Lesson 6, Prefixes (P. 10)

A. 1. disappear
2. unconcerned
3. unaware
4. discover
5. unharmed
6. dislike
7. disagree

B. 1. misunderstood
2. misuse
3. recreate
4. relive
5. misjudged
6. react

Lesson 7, Suffixes (P. 11)

A. 1. successful
2. tireless
3. effortless
4. careless
5. meaningful
6. endless
7. worthless
8. joyless

B. 1. without color
2. without a bottom
3. full of sorrow
4. full of beauty
5. without flavor

Lesson 8, Compound Words (P. 12)

A. 1. week, end
2. home, made
3. water, melon
4. sun, set

B. 1. tugboat
2. waterfront
3. loudspeaker
4. watchman
5. fireplace

C. Sentences will vary. Suggested compound words: newspaper, midnight, notebook, baseball

Lesson 9, Contractions (P. 13)

A. 1. I'll
2. we've
3. You'll
4. she's
5. he's

B. 1. can not
2. did not
3. will not
4. is not
5. we will

Review (P. 14)

A. Sentences will vary. Suggested synonyms:
1. big; little
2. scared; odd

B. 1. whole; entire
2. built; constructed

C. Answers will vary. Suggested antonyms:
1. large; hot
2. new; laugh

D. 1. wise
2. sad
3. sadden

E. 1. hear
2. two; to
3. It's; its
4. write; right
5. their; there

F. 1. moving air
2. to coil or turn

Review (P. 15)

G. Discuss your answers with your instructor.

H. 1. disagree; returning
2. thoughtless; misuse
3. thankful; unlimited

I. 1. air-conditioned
2. haircut
3. doorknob

J. 1. I would; I am
2. he is; does not
3. did not; she would

Using What You've Learned (P. 16)

A. Discuss your answer with your instructor.

B. **Line 2.** here; too
Line 3. to
Line 4. There
Line 5. It's
Line 6. two
Line 7. hear
Line 8. they're
Line 9. right

C. Discuss your answers with your instructor.

Using What You've Learned (P. 17)

D. 1. I am unhappy with the way the tape sounds.
2. I was hopeful that this tape would be good.
3. Now it seems that I misjudged it.
4. I'm still unsatisfied/dissatisfied with the way it sounds.

E. Sentences will vary. Suggested compound words: campfire, firelight, flashlight, postcard, flashcard, lightpost

F. 1. isn't   is not
2. wouldn't   would not
3. She's   She is
4. can't   can not
5. we're   we are

 Unit 2   Sentences

Lesson 10, Recognizing a Sentence (P. 18)

A. 1. S
2. S
4. S
5. S
8. S

B. 1. S
2. Discuss your answer with your instructor.
3. S
4. Discuss your answer with your instructor.
5. S

Lesson 11, Declarative and Interrogative (P. 19)

A. 1. interrogative
2. declarative
3. declarative
4. interrogative
5. declarative
6. interrogative
7. declarative
8. interrogative
9. declarative
10. interrogative
11. interrogative
12. declarative
13. interrogative
14. declarative
15. interrogative
16. interrogative
17. declarative
18. declarative

B. Discuss your answers with your instructor.

Lesson 12, Changing Sentences (P. 20)

A. 1. Am I finished?
2. Shouldn't you be finished?
3. Is this taking too long?
4. Are you leaving?
5. Can you stay?

B. Sentences may vary. Suggested:
1. Does Joe start his new job today?
2. Does he begin at nine o'clock?
3. Will he leave home at eight o'clock?
4. Does Joe like to work on cars?
5. Is repairing cars very interesting?
6. Is Joe sure he will like this job?
7. Will Joe do a good job?

Lesson 13, Imperative and Exclamatory (P. 21)

A. 1. imperative
2. imperative
3. exclamatory
4. imperative
5. exclamatory
6. exclamatory

---

7. imperative
8. imperative
9. exclamatory
10. exclamatory
11. imperative
12. imperative

B. Discuss your answers with your instructor.

Lesson 14, Subjects and Predicates (P. 22)

A. Discuss your answers with your instructor.

B. Discuss your answers with your instructor.

C. 1. subject
   2. predicate
   3. predicate
   4. subject
   5. predicate
   6. subject
   7. predicate

D. 1. Tennis was invented by Major Walter Wingfield.
   2. The game was called tennis-on-the-lawn.
   3. Mary Outerbridge brought the game to the United States.
   4. Tennis is a popular game.
   5. Venus Williams is a famous tennis player.
   6. You can play tennis, too.

Lesson 15, Simple Subjects and Predicates (P. 23)

A. The words in bold should be circled.
   1. The **plans** for a new car are made years ahead of time.
   2. Many important **decisions** go into the design of a car.
   3. Each **part** of the car is studied.
   4. A clay **model** is made to show what the car will look like.

B. The words in bold should be circled.
   1. Seven kinds of bears **live** in the world.
   2. Most bears **live** in areas north of the equator.
   3. Bears **have** small eyes.
   4. Bears **can live** as long as thirty years.
   5. A bear **uses** its claws to dig for food.
   6. Brown bears usually **eat** grasses, berries, and nuts.
   7. Seals and other animals **are** food for a polar bear.
   8. Most bears **sleep** all winter.
   9. Pandas **are** not really bears at all.

C.
	Subject	Predicate
1.	game	was played
2.	teams	played
3.	game	was

Lesson 16, Simple and Compound Sentences (P. 24)

A. 1. compound
   2. compound
   3. simple
   4. simple
   5. compound
   6. simple
   7. simple
   8. compound
   9. compound
   10. simple

B. Discuss your answers with your instructor.

Lesson 17, Combining Sentences (P. 25)

A. Sentences may vary. Suggested:
   1. We have to write a history report.
   2. My subject is the Civil War and Robert E. Lee.
   3. We must use the encyclopedia and other books.
   4. I should stop wasting time and start my report.

B. Sentences may vary. Suggested:
1. Juan bought a big, brown horse.
2. The horse is kept in an old, red barn.
3. Juan and Lynn ride the horse in a field.

C. Discuss your answers with your instructor.

Lesson 18, Avoiding Run-on Sentences (P. 26)

Answers may vary. Suggested:
1. One morning we found a baby bird.
2. It had been knocked from its nest by high winds.
3. Its mother was nowhere to be seen.
4. It was too young to fly.
5. We took it inside to care for it.
6. We were excited about taking care of the bird.
7. We didn't know what to do about feeding it.

Answers may vary. Suggested:
1. The bird's little mouth flew open so often that we could not find enough insects to feed it.
2. Then we found that the little bird liked dog food.
3. It also liked little bits of cooked egg yolk.
4. We even made some worms out of hamburger meat.

Review (P. 27)

A. 1. X
2. S
3. S
4. X

B. 1. Did Joseph fly to Boston?
2. interrogative
3. interrogative
4. Is taking the train slower?

C. 1. imperative
2. imperative
3. imperative
4. exclamatory
5. exclamatory

D. The words in bold should be circled.
1. My cousin **Lee plays** hockey for the Hawks.
2. **He practices** early every morning.
3. Hockey **players love** the sport.
4. **They play** even in the coldest weather.
5. The **game** of hockey **has** very dedicated players and fans.
6. **Players skate** madly around the rink.

Review (P. 28)

E. 1. compound
2. simple
3. simple
4. compound

F. Sentences may vary. Suggested:
Hank got up early. He reviewed his notes again. So, the test today would be easy for him.

G. Andrea likes baked chicken.

H. Sentences may vary. Suggested:
1. I was tired of moving.
2. My family had moved four times in the past three years.
3. Leaving my friends was always the hardest.
4. It's not easy to start over and make new ones.
5. Now we can stay put in a town that I like.

I. Discuss your answers with your instructor.

Using What You've Learned (P. 29)

A. 1. sentence
2. Discuss your answer with your instructor.
3. Discuss your answer with your instructor.
4. sentence

B. The stripes on it stand for the first thirteen colonies. The stars represent the fifty states. The colors have a meaning, too. White means freedom from wrong. Red stands for courage. Blue stands for fairness. Everything on the flag has a meaning.

1. How much do you know about the U.S. flag?
2. What do you think the stars stand for?
3. Did you know that?

C.
1. Did Jetta run to the grocery store?
2. Did she buy bread and milk?
3. Did she stop at the park?
4. Was Jetta surprised at how long she was gone?

D. Discuss your answers with your instructor.

Using What You've Learned (P. 30)

E. Fingerprints can prove who a person is. A light powder is used so fingerprints can be seen. Each person's fingerprints are different from anyone else's fingerprints. Even the fingerprints of twins are different. A person's fingerprints stay the same as he or she grows older.

1. Fingerprints   can prove
2. powder   is used
3. fingerprints   are
4. fingerprints   are
5. fingerprints   stay

F. Oranges are grown in Florida, and grapefruit are also grown there. Other fruits grow in Florida, but citrus fruit is still the main crop.

1. The main product of Florida is citrus fruit.
2. Citrus fruit needs warm weather to grow.
3. Many vegetables are also grown in Florida.

G. Sentences may vary. Suggested:
Flies are interesting insects. The eyes of a fly have up to 400 parts. They really see only motion and light. A fly has six legs and six feet. Each foot has a pair of claws.

Unit 3 Grammar and Usage

Lesson 19, Nouns (P. 31)

A.
1. Mrs. Smith has a big job ahead.
2. She needs to plan a picnic for her family.
3. Mrs. Smith must find a big park.
4. The family always enjoys the picnic.
5. It is a big event every year.
6. Mr. Smith is planning some games.
7. He will set up a net for volleyball.
8. Margie will make the hamburgers.
9. Mrs. Smith finally picked Riverview Park.
10. The park is on the Mississippi River.

B.
1. thing
2. person
3. person
4. place
5. person
6. thing
7. place
8. person
9. place
10. person
11. place
12. thing
13. person

Lesson 20, Proper and Common Nouns (P. 32)

A.
1. cousin, holidays
2. country
3. cousin; visitor
4. stories
5. year

B. **1.** Dr. Alvarado; New York
2. Parkside Hospital
3. September
4. Roosevelt University;
Queens, New York
5. United States

C. Discuss your answers with your instructor.

Lesson 21, Singular and Plural Nouns (P. 33)

A. **1.** S; porches
2. S; chairs
3. P; girl
4. S; wives
5. P; fly
6. S; skies
7. P; fox
8. P; half
9. S; pencils
10. S; alleys
11. P; leaf
12. S; pouches
13. P; inch
14. S; shelves

B. The words in bold should be circled.
1. plural **programs**
2. singular **hour**
3. singular **time**
4. singular **family**
5. plural **magazines**
6. singular **show**

Lesson 22, Singular Possessive Nouns (P. 34)

A. **1.** my aunt's house
2. my cousin's dog
3. my friend's books
4. my brother's bicycle
5. the cook's apron

B. **1.** Jerry's
2. officer's
3. thief's
4. automobile's
5. city's

C. **1.** store's
2. Lisa's
3. clerk's
4. bag's
5. man's

Lesson 23, Plural Possessive Nouns (P. 35)

A. **1.** sisters'
2. uniforms'
3. parents'
4. members'
5. instruments'

B. **1.** Farmers'
2. children's
3. ponds'
4. sheep's
5. cows'
6. barns'

Lesson 24, Action Verbs (P. 36)

A. **1.** jumped
2. leaped
3. snapped
4. spun
5. arched
6. pulled
7. danced
8. howled
9. licked
10. yawned
11. chewed
12. snarled
13. teased
14. pulled
15. snapped
16. shot
17. bounded
18. scrambled

B. Discuss your answers with your instructor.

Lesson 25, Linking Verbs (P. 37)

A. Linking verbs may vary. Suggested:
1. is
2. grow
3. smells
4. look
5. seem
6. taste
7. sound
8. become

B. 1. L
3. L
5. L
6. L

Lesson 26, Helping Verbs (P. 38)

The words in bold should be circled.
1. **had** wanted
2. **had** planned
3. **has** gone
4. **were** waiting
5. **was** raking
6. **were** looking
7. **couldn't** find
8. **were** forced
9. **was** given
10. **is** going
11. **has** gone
12. **had** told
13. **was** going
14. **had** planned
15. **am** going
16. **have** seen
17. **are** taking
18. **is** meeting
19. **is** riding
20. **are** looking

Lesson 27, Verb Tenses (P. 39)

A. 1. past
2. past
3. present
4. future
5. present
6. past
7. future
8. present
9. future
10. future
11. future

B. Discuss your answers with your instructor.

Lesson 28, Regular Verbs (P. 40)

A. 1. looked
2. gasped
3. settled
4. stepped
5. hurried
6. crushed
7. scratched
8. headed
9. changed
10. dropped

B. 1. sailed the boat
2. steered a straight course
3. carried the sail
4. enjoyed the fresh air and sunshine

Lesson 29, Irregular Verbs (P. 41)

A. 1. went
2. left
3. took
4. knew
5. grew
6. saw
7. gave
8. sat
9. came
10. flew
11. said
12. began
13. wrote
14. broke
15. threw
16. chose
17. fell
18. ran

Lesson 30, Making Subjects and Verbs Agree (P. 42)

1. eat; plural
2. lives; singular
3. fly; plural
4. feeds; singular
5. scratch; plural
6. cause; plural
7. destroys; singular
8. fight; plural
9. slows; singular
10. acts; singular
11. drop; plural
12. watches; singular
13. spread; plural
14. kills; singular
15. lose; plural
16. needs; singular
17. help; plural

Lesson 31, Subjects and Linking Verbs (P. 43)

A. Answers may vary. Suggested:
1. was
2. was
3. were
4. is
5. are
6. are
7. is
8. is

B. Answers may vary. Suggested:
1. There are
2. There were
3. There is
4. There are
5. There are
6. There is
7. There are
8. There is

Lesson 32, Subject Pronouns (P. 44)

A. 1. She
2. It
3. They
4. You
5. We
6. I
7. He
8. I

B. 1. I
2. We
3. He
4. It
5. They
6. you
7. She
8. I

C. Discuss your answers with your instructor.

Lesson 33, Object Pronouns (P. 45)

A. 1. it
2. us
3. me
4. us
5. them
6. you
7. him
8. me

B. 1. me
2. him
3. it
4. us
5. them
6. them
7. her
8. them

C. Discuss your answers with your instructor.

Lesson 34, Using Pronouns (P. 46)

1. We
2. They
3. It
4. them
5. us
6. He
7. him
8. she
9. her
10. us

Lesson 35, Possessive Pronouns (P. 47)

1. My
2. our
3. Its
4. My or Our
5. his
6. his
7. her
8. our
9. Your or My
10. your or my
11. their
12. his or our
13. her
14. her
15. Their, Her, or Its
16. our
17. its, his, or her
18. my or our
19. Its
20. your

Lesson 36, Adjectives (P. 48)

A.
1. big, tiny
2. sharp, bright
3. scared, small
4. speeding, wet
5. tired, dark
6. damp, big
7. little, wide

B. Answers may vary. Suggested:
Line 1. Many, beautiful
Line 2. sparkling
Line 3. dark; Wild
Line 4. green; Gentle
Line 5. fierce

Line 1. young or strong; wooden or shaky
Line 2. strong or soft; thick
Line 3. best or young; shaky or wooden
Line 4. six, red; soft
Line 5. bare

Lesson 37, Adjectives That Compare (P. 49)

A.
1. smallest
2. smaller
3. cutest
4. funnier
5. whitest
6. longest
7. naughtiest
8. harder
9. later
10. busier
11. happiest
12. biggest

B.
1. lighter
2. darkest
3. straighter
4. wildest
5. longer
6. shortest
7. longer
8. warmer
9. colder
10. coldest

Lesson 38, Adverbs (P. 50)

A.
1. widely, cheerfully
2. Yesterday, calmly
3. quickly, loudly
4. Later, quietly

B.
1. quietly, how
2. softly, how
3. Later; when
4. there, where

C. Answers may vary. Suggested:
1. quickly
2. there
3. Suddenly
4. brightly
5. anxiously
6. slowly
7. totally
8. hopelessly
9. quietly

Lesson 39, Adverbs That Compare (P. 51)

A. 1. faster
   2. later
   3. latest
   4. sooner
   5. most carefully
   6. harder

B. 1. later
   2. most quietly or quietest
   3. more loudly or louder
   4. more peacefully
   5. nearest
   6. more slowly or slower
   7. sooner
   8. more carefully

Lesson 40, Using Words Correctly (P. 52)

A. 1. well, good
   2. well
   3. good
   4. well
   5. well
   6. good
   7. well
   8. good
   9. good
   10. well
   11. good

B. 1. any
   2. any
   3. nothing
   4. ever
   5. any
   6. anything
   7. anybody

Lesson 41, Using Other Words Correctly (P. 53)

A. 1. those
   2. them
   3. them, them
   4. those
   5. them, those
   6. them
   7. those
   8. those

B. 1. don't
   2. doesn't
   3. doesn't
   4. doesn't
   5. don't, doesn't
   6. doesn't
   7. don't
   8. don't

Review (P. 54)

A. The words in bold should be circled. The words in italics should be boxed.
   1. Mark, **car**
   2. **town**, Chester
   3. Jan, **farm**
   4. **horse**, Bullet
   5. Bullet, *Jan's;* **pet**
   6. **horse**, **dogs**, **burro**
   7. **burro**, All Ears, *horse's*, **barn**
   8. *dogs'*, **home**, **porch**

B. 1. H
   2. A
   3. H
   4. L
   5. H
   6. L
   7. A
   8. A

C. 1. received
   2. will decide
   3. choose
   4. went
   5. likes
   6. grew

Review (P. 55)

D. 1. are
   2. There are
   3. follow
   4. used
   5. was
   6. There were
   7. were
   8. gave
   9. said
   10. are, added

E. 1. She, him
2. She, it
3. Her
4. He, it, it
5. She, he
6. They, their
7. She
8. he, it
9. his
10. she, he

F. The words in bold should be circled.
1. adjective; **movie**
2. adjective; **dazzling**
3. adjective; **wonderful**
4. adjective; **bigger**
5. adverb; **quickly**
6. adverb; **Later**
7. adverb; **harder**
8. adjective; **good**

Using What You've Learned (P. 56)

A. 1.

Common	Proper
house	Marty
idea	Charleston
history	Mr. Bremmer
people	
place	
door	

2. As he stood outside the old house, Marty wondered if this was a good idea. He wanted to go in, but the history of the house stopped him. All of the people in Charleston knew of Mr. Bremmer and this place. Marty started to walk toward the door. He still wondered if he should.

B. The words in bold should be circled.
1. Some jobs are not worth the money.
2. We agree with that.
3. Whoever watches this place must be brave.
4. Marty is not sure that he is brave enough.

Using What You've Learned (P. 57)

C. Marty got up <u>his</u> nerve and walked to the house. The front of <u>it</u> was dark. There were faces carved in the stone. <u>They</u> looked mean. "<u>Those/They</u> are strange," he thought. <u>They</u> scared <u>him</u>. "Oh well, here I go," <u>he</u> said to himself.

D. Answers may vary. Suggested:
1. rusty, slowly
2. scariest, ever
3. noisy, quieter
4. shaky, barely
5. brighter, strangely

E. Line 1. doesn't
Line 2. Those
Line 3. don't; ever
Line 4. anything
Line 5. well
Line 6. ever

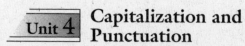

Unit 4 Capitalization and Punctuation

Lesson 42, Names of People and Pets (P. 58)
1. Uncle George got up early today.
2. He and Aunt Beth had a special job to do.
3. Uncle George and Aunt Beth were going to the animal shelter.
4. They wanted to find a puppy for Susan and Michael.
5. Uncle George and Aunt Beth thought a small dog would be nice.
6. But Susan and Michael wanted a big dog.
7. Uncle George saw a cute kitten named Mittens.
8. In the very last cage, they saw Sasha.
9. Uncle George and Aunt Beth loved her at once.
10. When Sasha ran circles around Michael, he loved her, too.

Lesson 43, Names of Places and Things (P. 59)

A. 1. Our family will spend Memorial Day in Washington.
2. We hope to see the White House and the Washington Monument.
3. We also want to see the Smithsonian Institution.
4. The Potomac River forms a border between Washington and Virginia.
5. The Lincoln Memorial is amazing to see at night.
6. The Vietnam Memorial gets many visitors.
7. There are many amazing sights in Washington.

B. Discuss your answers with your instructor.

Lesson 44, Capitalizing Titles (P. 60)

A. 1. Doctor William H. Black
2. Judge Rosa Allen
3. A Wrinkle in Time
4. Captain William Faircroft
5. The President of the United States
6. Doctor Laurie C. Bell
7. Attack of the Monster Plants
8. Major Carol Gates
9. Owls in the Family
10. My Side of the Mountain

B. 1. Mr. Thomas's
2. Judge George King
3. Judge King; Judge Claire Booth; Life in the Courts
4. Ms. Dias; Life in the Courts; Judge Booth
5. A Judge's Story; Raymond Field

Lesson 45, Capitalizing Abbreviations (P. 61)

A. 1. Tues.
2. Wed.
3. Thurs.
4. Fri.
5. Sat.
6. Sun.
7. Jan.
8. Nov.
9. Sept.
10. Aug.
11. Oct.
12. Dec.

B. 1. The conference is planned for Aug. 12.
2. It will be held in Wm. Taft Park.
3. George W. Bush will be there.
4. Our mayor, Ms. Foster, was pleased he could come.
5. Police Chief E. S. Rodriguez will introduce him.
6. Many people want to hear Mr. Bush speak.
7. They want to know how he likes life away from Washington, D.C.

Lesson 46, Parts of a Letter (P. 62)

7216 melvin street
houston, tx 77040
october 23 2006

dear fred,
I am doing a report on farm life. Do you have any information you can send me? My report must be turned in three weeks from today. I can really use any help you can give me. Pictures and facts would be helpful. The names of some books I could find at the library would also help a lot.

your friend,
jesse

820 w. state st.
lockhart, al 36455
october 29, 2006

dear jesse,
I'll be glad to help with your report. Better yet, why don't you come and visit? Call and let me know if you are coming. The library here serves all of alabama. I know we could find all the information you need.

your friend,
fred

Lesson 47, Sentences (P. 63)

A. The letters in bold should be circled.
1. **i** am going to ride my bike to the store.
2. **w**here is my bike?
3. **i**t is always in the garage by the hose.
4. **c**ould it be on the back porch?
5. **i**'ll ask Joanne if she has seen it.
6. **s**he said it was in the garage this morning.
7. **o**h, no, someone has stolen my bike!
8. **w**hat should I do now?
9. **w**ho could have taken it?

B. 1. I'll call the police about my bike.
2. Hurry, hurry, answer the phone!
3. Hello, is this the police station?
4. Yes, what can we do for you?
5. You must help me catch a bike thief.
6. How do you know your bike wasn't borrowed?

Lesson 48, Using Commas in Sentences (P. 64)

1. I called Juan, Janet, and Karen last Saturday.
2. Yes, they wanted to have a picnic.
3. Juan packed a lunch, and Karen brought a backpack.
4. Well, we were finally ready to go.
5. Yes, we found a perfect place by the beach.
6. We played volleyball, swam, and hiked.
7. It was a great picnic, and there were no ants around.
8. We collected shells, driftwood, and pebbles.
9. Juan cleaned up the garbage, and Karen packed the leftovers.
10. We sang, laughed, and read.

Lesson 49, Using Commas in Other Sentences (P. 65)

A. 1. Our neighbor, Buddy Rush, is gone.
2. Mr. Rush, his father, said he doesn't know where Buddy is.
3. Danny, did Buddy talk about going somewhere?
4. This seems very strange to me, Tim.
5. Chief Carter, our sheriff, thinks so, too.
6. Buddy, where are you?
7. Danny, don't you remember what I told you?
8. What should we do now, Chief Carter?

B. 1. X Someone is talking to Craig.
2. X Someone is talking to Lydia.
3. X Mrs. Hicks is our neighbor.
4. X Someone is talking to Carrie.
5. X Anna is my dog.

Lesson 50, Using Commas in Letters (P. 66)

A.
422 W. South St.
Dallas, TX 72843
November 12, 2006

Dear Mark,
  Thank you for coming to my party. It was fun having you there. I also want to thank you for the great sweatshirt. It fits fine, and I really like it.

Your friend,
Theresa

_____

8200 Columbus Ave.
Dallas, TX 72844
November 16, 2006

Dear Theresa,
  Don't forget about the trip to the museum on Saturday. See you there.

Sincerely,
Mark

B. 1. 321 Pebble Beach Drive
Jacksonville, FL 32211
November 17, 2006
2. 101 Main St.
Oakland, CA 10032
July 10, 2006

C. 1. Dear Rosa,
   2. Sincerely yours,
   3. Your friend,
   4. Dear Grandmother,
   5. Your grandson,
   6. Hi, Scott,

Lesson 51, Using Quotation Marks (P. 67)

1. "Do you want to talk about the interesting places we each visited this summer?" asked Ms. Chen.
2. "My sister and I visited my aunt in Nome, Alaska," said James. Or: James said, "My sister . . . Alaska."
3. "We flew to Quebec to see our grandmother," said Jenny. Or: Jenny said, "We flew . . . grandmother."
4. "We went to Arizona and saw the Grand Canyon," said Richard. Or: Richard said, "We went . . . Grand Canyon."

Lesson 52, More About Quotation Marks (P. 68)

1. "Well," said Mike, "Dot is just getting over a strange accident."
2. "What happened?" asked Susan.
3. "A thought struck her," said Mike.
4. Jake asked, "Why did you throw the alarm clock out the window?"
5. "Because," said Joan, "I wanted to see time fly."
6. "What did one wall say to another?" asked Bonnie.
7. "I'll meet you at the corner," answered David.
8. "What gets wetter," Carlos asked, "the more you dry?"
9. "A towel does," said Angie.
10. Mother said, "Are your feet dirty?"
11. "Yes," replied Bobby, "but don't worry because I have my shoes on."
12. Maria asked, "How can you tell when an ice cube is nervous?"
13. "It breaks out," said Bill, "in a cold sweat."
14. Anna asked, "What is black-and-white and red all over?"
15. "It's a blushing zebra," said Jake.
16. "What did the rug say to the floor?" asked Mike.
17. "Don't move," replied Bonnie, "because I've got you covered."
18. Joan asked, "Why do sponges do a good job?"
19. "They become absorbed in their work," said Carlos.
20. Angie asked, "Why is a pencil like a riddle?"
21. "Because," said Maria, "it's no good without a point."

Lesson 53, Apostrophes in Contractions (P. 69)

A. 1. she will
   2. We are
   3. they will
   4. I will
   5. She is
   6. We had

B. 1. It's;   we're
   2. You're;   we've
   3. I'm;   they'll
   4. didn't;   should've
   5. I'll;   we'll
   6. We're;   I'm

Lesson 54, Apostrophes to Show Possession (P. 70)

A. 1. brother's   **3.** Dad's   **5.** family's
   2. car's   **4.** sisters' **6.** friends'

B. 1. We all liked Jennifer's story the best.
   2. The story's setting was an old castle.
   3. There was a prison in the castle's basement.
   4. The students' attention was on Jennifer as she read.
   5. A cruel man lived in the castle's tower.
   6. The cruel man's children weren't allowed to play.

Review (P. 71)

A. The letters in bold should be circled.
  1. **m**arjorie took her horse, **b**laze, out for a ride.
  2. **s**he rode through **p**laceville to the **m**iller house.
  3. **m**r. **m**iller's mother, **j**udge **m**iller, was on the **s**upreme **c**ourt.
  4. **j**udge **m**iller served from **s**ept. 1960 to **a**ug. 1990.
  5. **h**er record was well-known in **w**ashington, **d**. **c**.
  6. **s**enator **h**iggins often went to her for advice.
  7. **m**arjorie and her friends loved to hear **j**udge **m**iller talk about her experiences.

B.

> 5780 W. Natchez
> Miles, VT 05857
> December 10, 2006

Dear Pam,

  It's been a long time since my last letter. How are you? Everything is fine here, but I really miss having you as a neighbor. Amy, our new neighbor, is nice. She goes to Taft School, and she is in my class. No, she will never replace you as my best friend. Oh, I almost forgot! Mrs. Tandy said, "Tell Pam hello for me." We all miss you a lot. Do you still think you can visit this summer?

> Your friend,
> Delia

C. 1. "Henry, stand by the door for a minute," said Scott.
  2. "What for?" asked Henry.
  3. "I want you to hold the door," answered Scott, "while I bring in this table."
  4. Henry asked, "Are you going to carry that by yourself?"
  5. "It's not very heavy," said Scott.
  6. "What are you going to do with it?" asked Henry.
  7. "We need it for the kitchen," said Scott.

Review (P. 72)

D. 1. "Well, it's time to get to work," said Lisa.
  2. Lisa walked out of the room, and Jeremy followed her.
  3. Lisa pointed to the trash can.
  4. "What a mess!" Jeremy cried.
  5. "Your dog did this," said Lisa.
  6. "Oh, so now Peanut's all mine," said Jeremy.
  7. "Yes, when he's bad, he's yours," said Lisa.
  8. They laughed and cleaned up the trash together.

E. 1. I'll see what needs to be done with dinner's leftovers.
  2. I think they're cool enough to put on the refrigerator's shelf.
  3. Dan hopes we're not going to have that for tomorrow's lunch.
  4. He doesn't think that his sister's daughters will eat it.
  5. He's wrong; cold pizza is his nieces' favorite food.
  6. They'll be happy with this lunch's surprise.

Using What You've Learned (P. 73)

A. The letters in bold should be circled.
  miriam **s**tone, WBZI's top reporter, woke up early. **s**he said, "I have plenty of time to get ready." **s**he thought of the letter she received yesterday:

> 920 **s**. **l**ake **st**.
> **k**ansas **c**ity, **mo** 43210
> **a**pril 1, 2006
>
> **d**ear **m**iriam,
>   **i**f you want a really exciting story, meet me at the **j**.**m**. **b**anister **l**ibrary at ten o'clock tomorrow morning. I'm sure your station's newsroom will want this story.
>
> > **y**ours truly,
> > A Fan

she asked herself what it could be. miriam dressed, ate breakfast, got her notebook, and headed for the library. it was not far, and soon she was there.

suddenly, a short woman in a dark dress walked up and said, "I wrote the letter." she said, "you must hear my story."

"my name is anna," she said. "I've been tricked by a gang of crooks. i need your help."

anna told miriam about a man named general j.c. cook who said he worked for the united states army. he told her he needed a key to all the safety boxes in the bank where she worked. "yes," she said, "it was strange, but he said it was for the country." now all of the boxes had been robbed, and she was sure it was general cook's work.

miriam was excited about the story. "now," said miriam, "tell me everything you can remember about general j.c. cook."

"wow, what a story!" miriam said excitedly.

Using What You've Learned (P. 74)

B.
420 Station St.
Park Ridge, IL 60010
April 3, 2006

Dear Mr. Thompson,

I appreciate the time you spent with me Tuesday. I learned a great deal about Thompson's Freight Lines, and I am sure that I would do a good job for your company. I have two years of experience in shipping goods around the world.

It was a pleasure to meet you and speak with you. What a surprise to learn that you know my Uncle Joe so well! He speaks very highly of you and your company.

Thank you again for seeing me. I'll call you in a few days.

Yours truly,
Wayne S. Carver

Unit 5 Composition

Lesson 55, Writing Sentences (P. 75)

1. a. yes; Nora
    b. yes; needed a hobby
    c. yes; yes
2. a. yes; Nora
    b. no; there isn't one
    c. no; no
3. a. no; there isn't one
    b. yes; will do a family history
    c. no; no
4. a. yes; Nora
    b. yes; began planning
    c. yes; yes
5. a. no; there isn't one
    b. yes; asked questions
    c. no; no

Lesson 56, Writing Topic Sentences (P. 76)

A. Nora decided that she needed a hobby.

B.   To get the information she needed, Nora would have to ask many questions. She thought about the kinds of questions she would ask. She wanted to make sure that she didn't forget any questions. So Nora wrote down a list of questions that she would ask each person. Next, she made copies of the list. She put one person's name at the top of each copy. Then she was ready to talk to people.

Lesson 57, Writing Supporting Details (P. 77)

Sentences 4, 5, and 8 should be crossed out.

Nora was ready to begin her history. First, she put her questions into a notebook. She made sure she had pens and extra paper. Then Nora called Grandpa Casey and asked when she could come and talk to him. She also called Grandpa Vargas. Both of her grandfathers were glad to help with the family history.

Lesson 58, Time Order in Paragraphs (P. 78)

Sentence order: 3, 4, 9, 7, 8, 1, 6, 2, 5, and 10

Lesson 59, Writing a Conversation (P. 79)

Paragraphs may vary. Suggested:

Nora asked, "What was it like when you were growing up?"

"I will tell you about my boyhood in Mexico," said Grandpa Vargas.

"My father raised sheep. I used to watch the flock of sheep," said Grandpa Vargas.

"It was not an easy job because wolves were always nearby," he said.

Nora said, "Please tell me about the wolves."

Lesson 60, Topic and Audience (P. 80)

A.
1. adult
2. child
3. teenager
4. adult
5. child
6. teenager
7. teenager
8. child
9. adult
10. child
11. adult

B. Discuss your answers with your instructor.

Lesson 61, Planning an Outline (P. 81)

Discuss your answers with your instructor.

Lesson 62, A Narrative Paragraph (P. 82)

1. Topic Sentence: "Ah," said Grandpa, "my meeting with the wolf was very exciting."
Time order words: Then, Next, Finally, Afterward

2. Answers may vary. Suggested:
They had just arrived at the meadow.
The sheep and Blanco were unsettled.
Blanco leaped on a sheep's back and raced across the flock.
The wolf attacked.
Blanco fought the wolf.
Grandpa yelled and swung the stick at the wolf.
The wolf left.
Grandpa and Blanco felt proud.

Lesson 63, Writing a Narrative Paragraph (P. 83)

Discuss your answers with your instructor.

Review (P. 84)

A.
1. sentence
2. She (Nora) could listen for hours.
3. sentence
4. She (Nora) wished her life was that interesting.

B. Nora wanted to make a lasting history of her family.

C. Sentence 4 should be crossed out.
Nora planned her recorded history. She read through her list of questions. Then she thought about how much time each would take to answer. Next, she went shopping for blank tapes. Finally, she was ready to let her grandfathers tell their stories.

Review (P. 85)

D. Conversations may vary. Suggested:
Nora asked, "How did you get to the United States, Grandpa Casey?"

"I came to Boston from Ireland by ship," said Grandpa Casey.

"Where is your favorite place?" asked Nora.

Grandpa Casey said, "I like it where I am right now."

E. Statement: Writing a narrative paragraph
  I. Choose a topic
  II. Write a topic sentence
  III. Write information about the topic
    A. Add supporting details
    B. Use time order words

F. The words in bold should be circled.
Grandpa's twin brothers played tricks on people. **First**, they'd dress exactly alike. Then they'd both answer when people said one of their names. **Finally**, they'd look at each other and laugh.

Using What You've Learned (P. 86)

A. Discuss your answer with your instructor.

B. Discuss your answer with your instructor.

C. Discuss your answer with your instructor.

Using What You've Learned (P. 87)

D. Discuss your answer with your instructor.

E. Discuss your answer with your instructor.

Unit 6 Study Skills

Lesson 64, Alphabetical Order (P. 88)

1. 3, 7, 1, 6, 5, 2, 8, 4
2. 6, 1, 7, 4, 2, 5, 8, 9, 3
3. 7, 6, 1, 8, 3, 2, 4, 5
4. 2, 8, 1, 6, 9, 4, 3, 5, 7
5. 1, 4, 8, 2, 6, 3, 5, 7
6. 9, 6, 3, 2, 7, 8, 4, 1, 5

Lesson 65, Dictionary: Guide Words (P. 89)

A. The following words should be circled:
  1. anxious
     amount
     arrest
     alive
     also
     ant
     allow
  2. fourth
     flower
     fog
     fly
     flame
     flew
     flight
  3. side
     shawl
     seventeen
     sink
     settle
     sign
     shelter

B. 1. lake / lead
     lake
     lamp
     lap
     last
     late
     lawn
     lead
2. pack / pat
     pack
     pad
     page
     palm
     pan
     pass
     pat

Lesson 66, Dictionary: Pronunciation (P. 90)

A. 1. girl
   2. lowly
   3. write
   4. trout
   5. glide
   6. huge
   7. gallop
   8. hug
   9. vanish

B. 1. word
 2. dictionary
 3. guide
 4. found
 5. respelling

Lesson 67, Dictionary: Definitions (P. 91)

A. 1. noun
 2. adjective
 3. verb
 4. folktale, follower, folly
 5. Discuss your answer with your instructor.

B. Discuss your answers with your instructor.

Lesson 68, Dictionary: Multiple Meanings (P. 92)

A. 1. 3; 3; 3
 2. 2; 5

B. 1. 1
 2. 2
 3. 1
 4. 1
 5. 3

Lesson 69, Using an Encyclopedia (P. 93)

A. 1. vitamins
 2. to keep your body healthy
 3. to get all the vitamins your body needs
 4. during periods of rapid growth, during stress, and while recovering from an illness
 5. minerals
 6. they both are needed by the body for good health
 7. no

Lesson 69, Using an Encyclopedia (P. 94)

B. 1. Mandela
 2. food
 3. United
 4. oceans
 5. Thatcher
 6. United
 7. games
 8. dogs

C. 1. 9   4. 16   7. 21
 2. 2   5. 13   8. 19
 3. 16   6. 2

Lesson 70, Parts of a Book (P. 95)

 1. Language Exercises for Adults, Level D
 2. page 31
 3. 3, 34, 35, 69, 70, 72, 73, 74, 107, 114
 4. 2006
 5. Saranna Moeller, Betty Jones, and Cynthia T. Strauch
 6. 10
 7. 88
 8. inside back cover
 9. 2, 50, 51, 55, 106, 113
 10. Lesson 30, Making Subjects and Verbs Agree
 11. 2, 36, 54, 104, 113
 12. Harcourt Achieve Inc.
 13. Lesson 59, Writing a Conversation

Review (P. 96)

A. fruit   pizza
 morning   ran
 onion   wag

B. 1. debt   2. demand
 deck   den
 defend   depend
 degree   design

C. 1. need
 2. dictionary
 3. say
 4. sentence

D. 1. verb
 2. ours
 3. chuck
 4. chuck

Review (P. 97)

E. 1. Mark Twain
 2. 1910
 3. The Adventures of Huckleberry Finn
 4. Hannibal, Missouri
 5. It is his real name.

F.
1. computers, 1
2. Einstein, 2
3. Amazon, 1
4. Norway, 5
5. Romania, 6
6. eagles, 2

G.
1. title page
2. title page
3. index
4. copyright page
5. table of contents
6. copyright page

Using What You've Learned (P. 98)

A. Discuss your answers with your instructor.

B.
1. noun
2. Discuss your answer with your instructor.
3. Discuss your answer with your instructor.
4. Discuss your answer with your instructor.

Using What You've Learned (P. 99)

C. Discuss your answers with your instructor.

1. ache
2. ancient
3. blizzard
4. disease
5. helpful
6. howl
7. magician
8. remind
9. scent
10. venture

D. Discuss your answers with your instructor.

 Final Reviews

Final Review, Unit 1 (P. 100)

1. smiled, grinned
2. ran, dashed
3. spoke, talked

1. wrong
2. remembered
3. sad

1. hear
2. too
3. It's
4. they're
5. two, right
6. there
7. write
8. Its, here
9. their
10. too, to

1. take up a weapon
2. noise a dog makes
3. ran quickly

Final Review, Unit 1 (P. 101)

1. P   2. P   3. S   4. S   5. P

1. straw, berries
2. rattle, snake
3. sand, paper

1. it's
2. couldn't
3. they'll
4. I'm
5. won't

The words in bold should be circled.
  Many people think **he's** gone to the **seashore**. But they're wrong. He'd rather go to his **mountaintop hideaway**. He'll stay there until **somebody** gets worried. Then they'll remember and call him there. He won't let **anything** but an emergency make him come back until he's ready!

Final Review, Unit 2 (P. 102)

1. X   2. X   3. S   4. S
5. X   6. S   7. S   8. X

1. interrogative
2. exclamatory
3. imperative
4. declarative
5. interrogative
6. declarative
7. declarative
8. exclamatory

1. predicate
2. subject
3. predicate
4. subject

The words in bold should be circled.
1. For years **factories** dumped wastes into lakes and rivers.
2. Some waste **materials** cause no harm.
3. Other **waste** poisoned the water.
4. Today many **factories** protect the water from wastes.

Final Review, Unit 2 (P. 103)

1. compound   **3.** simple   **5.** simple

2. simple   **4.** compound   **6.** compound

Answers may vary. Suggested:

1. Jessie went fishing, and Ted went swimming.
2. Yesterday was cold, but today is a rainy, gray day.
3. Canada and the United States are neighbors, and they are friends.

Paragraphs may vary. Suggested:

My grandmother was a pioneer. She traveled by wagon train to Missouri. When she turned 12, she decided she wanted to ride a horse. Her father told her she couldn't do that in a skirt. So she had her mother make her some pants. She wanted to be on her own. She wanted more freedom. She kept a diary, and I've read it all. That's how I know.

Final Review, Unit 3 (P. 104)

The words in bold should be circled.

1. <u>Sally</u> sat next to the **window**.
2. It was a wonderful **morning** in <u>June</u>.
3. Warm **mornings** in <u>California</u> are very beautiful.

1. dog's   **2.** puppies'   **3.** dogs   **4.** tails

1. A   **2.** A   **3.** H   **4.** A   **5.** H   **6.** L

1. present   **2.** future   **3.** past

1. plural, are   **3.** singular, is
2. plural, read   **4.** singular, likes

Final Review, Unit 3 (P. 105)

1. P; Her job is park ranger.
2. S; She loves spending every day in the forest.
3. O; Her favorite thing is walking among them.
4. P; She really likes it when their leaves change.
5. P; Ed sometimes brings his camera to take pictures.
6. P; Its pictures are clear and sharp.

1. adverb   **3.** adjective   **5.** adverb
2. adjective   **4.** adjective   **6.** adverb

1. don't   **3.** good   **5.** doesn't   **7.** well
2. ever   **4.** them   **6.** those

Final Review, Unit 4 (P. 106)

328 N. State St.
New York, NY 10010
January 2, 2006

Dear Dr. Turner,

I want to thank you for your kindness to Tootsie, my pet bird. My friend, Jack, said, "No one knows how to cure birds. They're different from other types of pets. You shouldn't waste your money." Can you believe that? I didn't agree with Jack, so I brought Tootsie to your office. Thanks to you, Tootsie is fine again.

Sincerely,
Carlos Gomez

Final Review, Unit 4 (P. 107)

1. "Our next topic," said Mr. Lopez, "will be the fall of the Roman Empire."
2. "Hurry and get out of there!" cried Louis.
3. Ted, please don't ask me to do that.
4. "Has the jury reached a verdict?" asked Judge Mallory.
5. Eric said, "I'll be the first to tell you if you're right."
6. Well, I guess it's all right.
7. We spent the day swimming, hiking, and having a picnic.

1. Didn't you see the look on Dean's face?
2. It's pretty clear he doesn't like our plan.
3. He hasn't said anything at all about Frank's idea.
4. We're going to have to make up our minds soon.
5. The men's ideas are different from ours.
6. Everyone's ideas should be considered.

Final Review, Unit 5 (P. 108)

The words in bold should be circled.

<u>Forests grow in a cycle</u>. **First**, the strongest trees grow very large. **Then** the other trees cannot get enough sunlight. Weaker trees either stay short or die. **Afterward**, new growth begins. Sometimes fires destroy a whole forest.

Conversations will vary. Suggested:

"Chris, did you understand the movie?" asked Bob.

"I'm not sure," Chris said. "I thought I did at first, but then I got confused."

"I did, too," said Bob.

"What did you think of it, Bob?" asked Chris.

Bob said, "I liked it, but I wondered about the ending?"

Chris said, "The writer was probably as confused as we were!"

Final Review, Unit 5 (P. 109)

Statement: Cowboys in the Old West

I. Equipment
  A. Saddle and bridle
  B. Gun and rope
II. Clothing

Paragraphs will vary. Suggested:

Judy had planned her day well. Tonight she would invite her parents over for dinner. First, she cleaned her entire house. She chose the clothes she would wear. Next, she went to the florist and bought a blue glass vase. Then she bought a beautiful bunch of flowers. She took the vase and flowers back home and put them on the table. After that, she went shopping for a special meal. Finally, she prepared the meal and waited for her parents to arrive.

Final Review, Unit 6 (P. 110)

rich / rock
  1. rich
  2. right
  3. rinse
  4. rob
  5. rock

baby / bat
  1. baby
  2. back
  3. ball
  4. base
  5. bat

Discuss your answers with your instructor.
1. adjective
2. 5
3. adjective, verb
4. a. verb, 2
   b. adjective, 2
   c. adjective, 1

Final Review, Unit 6 (P. 111)

1. the elbow
2. a joint between the upper and lower arm
3. it allows the arm to bend, twist, and turn
4. arm and wrist
5. no, only arm is mentioned

1. sea, 7
2. Hong, 3
3. nursing, 5
4. fly, 2
5. Keller, 4
6. aluminum, 1
7. vampires, 8
8. horses, 3
9. Shakespeare, 7
10. boomerangs, 1
11. instruments, 3
12. new, 5

1. table of contents
2. index
3. title page
4. copyright page

Check What You've Learned (P. 112)

A. 1. H   2. S   3. A   4. S
B. 1. a student
C. 1. C   2. P   3. S   4. S
D. 1. I'd   2. They'll
E. 1. IN   2. E   3. IM   4. D
F. 1. He / asked me a question.
   2. I / did not have an answer.

Sentences may vary. Suggested:

G. I watched a new show on television.

H. The wind blew over the trash can. I cleaned up the mess.

Check What You've Learned (P. 113)

I. The words in bold should be circled. The photographs of **Mary** in the show were some of **Rick's** best.

J. children's

K. 1. L   **2.** A   **3.** H

L. 1. present   **2.** future   **3.** past

M. 1. grow   **2.** needs

N. 1. their   **2.** we

O. The words in bold should be circled.
Yesterday I stepped **carefully** around the <u>sleeping</u> dog.

P. 1. well   **2.** Don't, any

Check What You've Learned (P. 114)

Q.
                    707 S. Baywood St.
                    Sacramento, CA 90034
                    Feb. 10, 2006
Dear Sally,
  When are you and Dave coming for a visit?
I can't wait to show you my new house! The
neighborhood's got everything I need. I really
love it here!
                    Your friend,
                    Todd

R. The words in bold should be circled.
  I decided to raise a vegetable garden. **First,**
I prepared the soil. **Then** I planted the seeds.
Finally, I watered the seeds.

S. Statement: Raising a vegetable garden
  I. Planting
     A. Prepare the soil
     B. Plant and water the seeds

Check What You've Learned (P. 115)

T. 1. noun
   2. cork
   3. corn / couch

U. 1. The Great Depression
   2. Herbert Hoover